GROWING UP WITH IRELAND

In a long career as a reporter working in newspapers, radio and television, Valerie Cox has interviewed people from every county in Ireland. Over eleven years working on RTÉ Radio's *Today* programme, she travelled around the country covering diverse news and local issues. She was out with the rescue services in floods and snow, and covered the events that make rural Ireland special, including the Ploughing Championships.

She is the author of three books, *Searching*, which tells the story of Ireland's missing people, *The Family Courts* and *A Ploughing People*.

Valerie lives in rural County Wicklow with her husband Brian – the couple have five grown-up children and four grandchildren.

Growing Up With Ireland

A Century of Memories from our Oldest and Wisest Citizens

Valerie Cox

HACHETTE
BOOKS
IRELAND

First published in Ireland in 2019 by
HACHETTE BOOKS IRELAND
First published in paperback in 2020

1

Cataloguing in Publication Data is available from the British Library

Paperback ISBN 978 1 52933 738 9

Typeset in Sabon by redrattledesign.com

Printed and bound in Great Britain by
Clays Ltd, Elcograf S.p.A

Hachette Books Ireland policy is to use papers that are natural, renewable
and recyclable products and made from wood grown in sustainable forests.
The logging and manufacturing processes are expected to conform to the
environmental regulations of the country of origin.

Hachette Books Ireland
8 Castlecourt Centre
Castleknock
Dublin 15, Ireland

A division of Hachette UK Ltd
Carmelite House, 50 Victoria Embankment, London EC4Y 0DZ

www.hachettebooksireland.ie

For my grandchildren, Brian, Henry, Ellie and Michael – children whose lives of freedom, dreaming and adventure have been made possible by those just separated from us by gossamer threads of laughter and love.

Contents

Introduction 1

1920: Major Events 11

Bringing Home the Christmas, Martin Keaveny 15

1921: Major Events 35

Romance at the Crossroads, Tom O'Mahony 39

A First Election, Anne Blake 46

Memories of the 1921 Troubles, Patrick Melinn 54

A Rambling House, Kevin Kealy & Sr Máire Kealy 68

Catching Roses, Anne Kennedy 102

1922: Major Events 127

To School on the Pony and Trap, Tom Stack
  & Sr Dympna Stack 131

The Shoe on the Anvil, Bridget Josephine Maguire 150

1923: Major Events 163

A Huguenot Legacy, Charlie Fitzmahony 167

The Bell-Ringer, Cyril Galbraith 178

1924: Major Events 195

The Loveliest Butter, Dorothy Talbot 197

Civil War and Heartbreak, Marie Elliott 214

1925: Major Events 233

A Fair Day to Remember, John Flanagan 235

A Missionary Life, Sr Cosmas Cullen 244

1926: Major Events 255

A Pulpit for Haughey, Denis O'Callaghan 259

The Best of Linen, Rose Smith 275

Saving Michael Collins, Nora Ryan 285

Gathering the Hay, Sabina Tierney 299

1927: Major Events 305

The Birth of a New Ireland, Eithne Lee &
  Maree O'Leary 308

Overcoming Religious Division, Pauline Hilliard 331

Spreading the Turf, James Mullin 345

1928: Major Events 349

Memories of Eviction, Michael O'Connell 353

1929: Major Events 365

A Border Crossing, Austin Dawe 369

Acknowledgements 385

Introduction

My father, Desmond FitzPatrick, was born in Dublin in 1922, the year the Irish Free State was established. He was one of eight children of Terence FitzPatrick and Mary Hackett and he grew up on Killeen Road in Rathmines.

When he was fifteen, he went to work for the Electricity Supply Board in the Pigeon House in Ringsend. His father was employed there too and Terence brought his young son along to what was almost the family firm as three of his other sons also worked there. I can remember my father's description of that first day cycling down through Ringsend towards the sea. He said he and his dad were almost smothered by the smoke coming from the Pigeon House and had to wrap handkerchiefs around their faces.

My grandfather, my father and three of my uncles, Jack, Terry and Gerry, spent most of their working lives in the ESB. When my father was in his twenties, most of his workmates started families. On the night shift, they would bring their babies' terry nappies to work and dry them overnight in the great heat from the furnaces. I remember as a young child being taken to see those fires through a thick glass and wondering was I peering into hell!

My father, who was just a little younger than my oldest interviewee, died in 2007, but writing this book and meeting so many other men and women of a similar age to him has made me realise that we are only ever a handshake from history.

Des FitzPatrick, age 2.

The people I've met, now in their nineties, can remember those born in the nineteenth century, a magical link with our communal past.

Between 1920 and 1929, 612,711 babies were born in Ireland –

ESB babies: Des, Gerry, Jack and Terry FitzPatrick.

314,505 male and 298,206 female – of whom about 22,237 are alive today.

From 1920, roughly sixty thousand babies were born each year, the boys slightly outnumbering the girls year by year. Of these births, between 725 and 815 sets of twins were born each year, and five to seven sets of triplets.

We can see from the most recent census, taken in 2016, that 318 of those born in 1920 are still alive, 450 from 1921, 734 from 1922, 1,210 from 1923, 1,551 from 1924, 2,067 from 1925, 2,733 from 1926, 3,418 from 1927, 4,378 from 1928 and 5,378 from 1929.

In reality, the figures for those still living are probably higher as, during the decades following the 1920s, there was mass emigration and, no doubt, some of those who emigrated are still alive in their adopted countries. For example, in 1923 the estimated figure for those who emigrated was 20,570 to places as diverse as the USA, Canada, Australia, New Zealand, South Africa and India, and they are just the destinations on record. Today, the surviving emigrants will appear in the statistics of their adoptive countries but they have no link to Irish statistics.

It has been a privilege to write this book, to meet so many men and women who have shared their stories with me, to listen to their sorrows and joys, to look at the photos of their grandchildren and their great-grandchildren, and to hear the wisdom of their long lives and their hopes for the future. From them, there was warmth and kindness and homemade scones and cups of tea and warm fires that stirred their memories.

Many of my interviewees live in their own homes. Others live in independent apartments or in nursing homes. Ten are still driving and two are still working.

Let's meet them!

Martin Keaveny himself an inventor, recalls the mass exodus from Glenamaddy in the 1930s. 'The Second World War started on 3 September and, on 6 October, a liner was making a last stop in Galway Bay to take US citizens and recent emigrants back home.'

Tom O'Mahony from Ballylanders in County Limerick remembers walking barefoot to school in summer and winter, and bringing sixpence for fuel to keep the fire going.

Anne Blake, widow of the late councillor Vincent Blake in County Wicklow, remembered 'putting out the cows and walking up the road and crying because they wanted him to go for election'.

Patrick Melinn who is still hands on at Melinn & Sons, the company he founded eighty years ago.

Vet **Kevin Kealy** and his sister **Sr Máire Kealy** recall their 'rambling house' in Wolf Hill in County Laois and growing up without electricity.

Anne Kennedy's romance with her bus driver husband, Frank, began when he started throwing roses from his bus as she cycled along on her bicycle!

Siblings **Tom Stack** and **Sr Dympna Stack** from Moyvane in County Kerry tell how their IRA father James had to go on the run on his own wedding day and, speaking of the Tuam Mother and Baby Home, Sr Dympna notes, 'All virgin births! No word about a dad or the families.'

Bridget Maguire came from Drimeyra, near Ballinasloe in County Galway. Her father, Thomas Larkin, was the local blacksmith. 'I can still see him turning the shoe on the anvil, beating it out to size.'

Charlie Fitzmahony remembers watching de Valera as a child when he spoke in the Square in Portarlington as he campaigned in the first election following independence in February 1932.

Cyril Galbraith tells how, as a teenager, he went on a school exchange trip to Dresden in Germany, just before the outbreak of the Second World War. Cyril is now Ireland's oldest practising campanologist.

Dorothy 'Dot' Talbot was also on that Dresden trip and retired just this year as warden of her local Church of Ireland in County Clare.

Marie Elliott, the little girl 'with rosy cheeks and a Paris accent', remembers that Archbishop John Charles McQuaid stopped her Catholic school team from playing hockey against Protestant schools.

John Flanagan, who worked for the Automobile Association on the border, recalls the smuggling that went on – in both directions!

Sr Cosmas Cullen says she wanted to be a missionary sister from the time she made her First Communion.

Denis O'Callaghan, violinist and private secretary to Charles J. Haughey, remembers those eventful Haughey years.

Rose Smith from Oldcastle in County Meath tells how her mother made beautiful linen sheets from used flour bags, and how she kept for another set for visiting American family and for laying out the dead.

Nora Ryan tells of her father's friendship with Michael Collins and how he built a secret room in their attic in Riddlestown, County Limerick that Collins used when he was on the run.

Sabina Tierney remembers food rationing during the Second World War. 'There was only brown flour, some could make cakes out of it. My mother used to sift it with the white flour. It was like pig food but people had to make do with it.'

Maree O'Leary and **Eithne Lee** chose to be interviewed together. Eithne's family farm stood where Dublin airport is now, the land acquired through a compulsory purchase order, and Maree remembers her father telling her how he learned Irish from Sinéad de Valera.

Pauline Hilliard recalls how she and her husband Hugh won the pools while living in England and were able to buy their house in Ireland and return home.

James Mullin lived in New Zealand and became acquainted with Frederick Foster, one of the last people to be executed in that country.

Michael O'Connell was a 'Cork City young fella' who joined the civil service and says, 'Being appointed to Castlebar in 1945 was like being sent to America!'

Austin Dawe's father Felix was the vice-commander of a battalion of the IRA in Dundalk, County Louth. Austin remembers that time, and tells me about his experiences on the Lough Derg pilgrimage.

1920: Major Events

World

- First General Assembly of the League of Nations in Geneva

- In America, the 19th Amendment, giving women the right to vote, is signed into law by President Woodrow Wilson

- F. Scott Fitzgerald publishes his debut novel, *This Side of Paradise*

Ireland

- The Sinn Féin Lord Mayor of Cork Tomás Mac Curtain is murdered by armed and disguised RIC men who break into his home

- British recruits to the RIC begin to arrive in Ireland and become known as the Black and Tans from the colour of their uniforms

- Pope Benedict XV beatifies Oliver Plunkett

- The IRA orders a boycott of the RIC and their families

- Kingstown Urban District Council resolves to revert to the town's historic name of Dún Laoghaire

- Protestants expel Catholic workers from the Harland and Wolff shipyard in Belfast; two days later fourteen die and one hundred are injured in rioting in the city

- The formation of the Ulster Special Constabulary, an armed (and predominantly Protestant) police reserve, is announced

- Terence MacSwiney, Lord Mayor of Cork, dies in Brixton Prison on the seventy-fourth day of his hunger strike

- An eighteen-year-old medical student, Kevin Barry, is executed in Mountjoy Prison for participating in the killing of three young unarmed British soldiers

- The Irish Republican Army, on the instructions of Michael Collins, shoots dead fourteen British undercover agents in Dublin; in retaliation, the Auxiliary Division of the RIC opens fire on a crowd at a GAA football match in Croke Park, killing thirteen spectators and one player, and wounding sixty

- Martial law is declared in counties Cork, Kerry, Limerick and Tipperary

- The Burning of Cork: British forces set fire to the centre of Cork City, including City Hall, in reprisal for the death of a British auxiliary who had been killed in a guerrilla ambush

- The Government of Ireland Act 1920 is passed by the parliament of the United Kingdom and receives royal assent from George V, providing for the partition

of Ireland into Northern Ireland
and Southern Ireland with separate
parliaments, granting a measure of home
rule

- La Scala Theatre and Opera House in
  Dublin is opened as a cinema

- Actress Maureen O'Hara is born

- All-Ireland champions: Dublin (hurling)
  and Tipperary (football)

Bringing Home the Christmas
Martin Keaveny
Born 1 June 1920

Mary Gannon, mother of eleven children, died when her youngest, Martin Keaveny, was just five years old – her husband Michael was a widower for forty-five years.

Mary and Martin Keaveny with ten of their eleven children, Mark, Agnes, Moira, Margaret, Michael, John, Oona, Nell, Kate and Sally, 1924.

Martin's siblings later scattered all over the world – Mark, Agnes, Moira and Margaret to the USA, Michael, John, Oona and Nell to South Africa and Kate and Sally to the UK. But although he travelled and worked in the UK when he was a young man, Martin returned to Ireland to farm and raise a family, and he now resides at the Central Park Nursing Home in Clonberne, Ballinasloe in County Galway.

He tells me he drove a car until two years ago, when he was ninety-seven, and he still remembers the first one he owned, a Morris Minor. 'I think it was six months old when I got it. There wasn't much traffic then in Glenamaddy (County Galway) and there was only one other car in the village.' Martin also recalls his first tractor, a red Farmall Cub, which he got in 1954.

He loves both the Irish language and the work of the blind poet Antoine Ó Raifteirí and he greets me with a robust recitation *as Gaeilge*. '*Is Mise Raifteirí an file, Lán dúchais is grádh, Le súile gan solas, Le ciúnas gan crá.*' The last of the wandering poets is buried in Craughwell and Martin has visited his grave.

Martin, who is now in his centenary year, is also an inventor and a writer, and he gives me copies of some of the memories he has penned to use in our interview. He was a regular contributor to *Solas* magazine, which was the local parish publication for Glenamaddy, where Martin and his family grew up in a thatched farmhouse.

One of Martin's earliest memories is of a neighbour called Kate Scally, a dressmaker. 'I heard stories from my brothers and sisters of the great fun they had at school. I was told that I could go when the cuckoo would come, but that if I was too cross, I wouldn't be let go. So I did my best to behave.'

At that time, as Patrick Kavanagh's mother said, boys were not put into trousers until they were able to manage their buttons. 'I wore a frock up until then. The first preparation was to get a trousers made. I went to Kate, who lived in a small cottage. She was an old lady who wore silver-rimmed glasses on the top of her nose. She took my measurements but she wasn't very accurate. It was neither a long trouser nor a short one. The material used was corduroy. I was ready for school then.'

He also recalls his schoolteachers, Mr O'Dea and Mrs Treacy. 'Mr O'Dea described me as a boy with a good sense of humour.' But on his first day, Martin changed his mind about going to school and remembers trying to escape. 'When we were let out for play, I stole off, making my way home. I was halfway over the graveyard when I met two girls coming down from the chapel. They turned me round and landed me back in prison again. I didn't put up any resistance. I didn't attempt any other escape.'

About a dozen boys from the workhouse attended Glenamaddy school. They were seated on a long form along the wall. They were what we now call segregated. They didn't join in any games with the other children.

Martin has a photographic memory of those early schooldays. 'At first we were given trays of sand and then we got slates and chalk and plasticine. About a dozen boys from the workhouse attended Glenamaddy school. They were seated on a long form along the wall. They were what we now call segregated. They didn't join in any games with the other children. There was one big fellow called Mathias and he was in charge of the others and he carried a basketful of sandwiches and milk. They were all dressed the same in a grey uniform. They were well looked after. They moved to Tuam in 1927 and were later adopted by local families.'

Bringing Home the Christmas

Almost one hundred years ago, the highlight of a child's year was Christmas. Martin recalls his neighbours setting out for Glenamaddy with the jennet and cart early on the morning of 9 December to 'bring home the Christmas'. This date was chosen to avoid the rush closer to the big day. 'We looked forward to their return in the evening because Mary always bought a good supply of raisins and shared some of them out among the children in the village.'

On the Wednesday before Christmas, there was the 'big market day' when everyone came to town. 'Ass and carts competed for parking spaces. It was the day when farmers' wives sold their poultry. You could buy a fat goose for half a crown, and a turkey, chicken or duck for a shilling and sixpence. Potatoes cost three pence a stone and a cart load of turnips would set you back two shillings and sixpence. Money was scarce but people got by just the same. It was the time of year when family members who had emigrated to America came to the rescue with the few welcome dollars.

'As children, we were more interested in the big Christmas stocking displayed in Collins' shop window. A Christmas stocking measuring three feet long could be bought for a shilling. The price was beyond the reach of an individual so we sometimes clubbed our pennies together and bought one. On Christmas Day, we would rise early and head for seven-thirty mass. We set out at seven o'clock in the pitch dark. Usually there was hard frost and the ice cracked underfoot as we walked over cow tracks. Sometimes, we took the short route through cutaway bog and kicked clods to watch glow worms light up. On the high road, we might come across a shattered porter jar where someone had slipped on the icy road the previous night.'

The Second World War started on
3 September and, on 6 October,
a liner was making a last stop in
Galway Bay to take US citizens back
home. I accompanied my sister to
Tuam to catch the Galway train. My
brother John emigrated to England
the following day.

Looking for Work in the War Years

Most of the young people in the Glenamaddy area emigrated when they were about eighteen but they came home sometimes for holidays. 'I remember the day in 1939 when my sister Margaret, who had been home on a three-month visit, was returning to the United States. The Second World War started on 3 September and, on 6 October, a liner was making a last stop in Galway Bay to take US citizens back home. I accompanied my sister to Tuam to catch the Galway train. My brother John emigrated to England the following day.

'There was no work available locally, so, in February 1940, myself and Sarah Garvey, a neighbour, walked to Glenamaddy and took a taxi to Ballymoe railway station. We caught the mail boat to Holyhead and a train to Birmingham. I tried for a job clearing snow but was unsuccessful. It was about a fortnight before any work emerged. The digs I stayed in were very poor; I had to sleep in an attic. I felt perished. I eventually secured a job on the railway. It was very dirty work which involved carrying railway lines. The frost was still very hard. I teamed up with my brother Mark and together we headed by train to south Wales in search of better employment. I was to work as a carpenter. The job we went to had the same foreman that we had worked for before on the railway and he knew that I wasn't a qualified carpenter. The game was up and we returned to a snowy Birmingham.

'Next day we took the train to Stafford and we got work there as carpenters. Stafford was a nice place and we made many friends. After a while, we were transferred to Coventry which, by comparison, was terrible – all work and no play.

'By now the war had taken a bad turn. The English army was evacuated from Dunkirk. The canteen we used was in a huge building and every second person had a rifle with a fixed bayonet strapped to his back. The Germans were expected to invade at any moment. I applied for a visa to return home – at that time it was extremely difficult to get one. I said a lot of prayers and was eventually granted my passport to freedom. In England everywhere was blacked out. Air-raid sirens blared and people frantically dashed to the safety of the shelters. When I reached Holyhead, I was handed a life-jacket to wear on the crossing to

Dublin. It was the happiest day of my life when I set foot on Irish soil again.'

Glenamaddy Fair

Much of the social life in rural Ireland revolved around the fair, and the fair in Glenamaddy was one of the biggest in the country, having been held for the first time on 5 November 1889, when Martin's father was a young man. 'It catered for pigs, sheep and cattle. The first animal sold was a fat sow owned by Captain Keaveney. He got five sovereigns for the sow and five sovereigns for having sold the first animal. Ten sovereigns would be about €1,750 in today's money.

'My father sold pigs at the fair and, until 1930, those pigs were transported to Castlerea and Tuam railway stations by horse and cart. The carters were paid half a crown per pig for providing transport to Tuam and two shillings to Castlerea. Twenty horse carts, each carrying five pigs, would travel in convoy. The first lorries with single floors replaced the carts in 1930. There weren't any tags on the ears of the cattle at that time. Buyers would cut their initials on the beasts' rumps with a scissors so they could identify them as theirs.

There weren't any tags on the ears of the cattle at that time. Buyers would cut their initials on the beasts' rumps with a scissors so they could identify them as theirs.

'Fr Walter Conway ruled that the primary schools would remain closed on cattle fair days as it was considered dangerous for children to have to pass close to unenclosed animals. There was much amusement after the cattle were sold and paid for. Ballad singers sang songs and sold bundles of ballads after performing. There were matchmakers, cheap-jacks (salesmen) and delph men.

'Every household had a current edition of *Old Moore's Almanac* which listed all the fairs of Ireland. Twenty-four fairs were held in Glenamaddy each year.'

Farming Before the Tractor

When Martin was growing up, the farm work was interspersed with cutting turf on the bog. 'I brought home the turf with a horse and cart. It was thirsty work. We had a drink called fire water

– it was oaten meal in a can the sweets came in and it was good for the thirst on a hot day.'

But this was before the advent of the tractor. 'We used ploughs and the bodies of the first ploughs were made from wood. Very few people had horses so they had to hire ploughmen to do the work. People got jennets and they were able to draw the plough. Neighbours joined together to form teams. Jennets were very useful animals as they were nearly as strong as horses but a lot easier to maintain. At one time there were eleven jennets and only four horses in Esker in County Galway. There were good ploughmen and bad. You could whistle or sing while ploughing – it was a satisfying job. Opening the first furrow was the most difficult part of ploughing a field. The last furrow was called a *caológ*.'

We had a drink called fire water – it was oaten meal in a can the sweets came in and it was good for the thirst on a hot day.

The Mill and the Flax

When Martin returned from England he settled on a dairy farm with his family, where he was a successful farmer, winning prizes for the quality of his silage. He was also very much involved in the local mill, where he had helped his father from the age of ten.

He remembers one cold November day around 1930. 'My father loaded a big pile of bags of oats onto the horse cart bound for Gilmore's mill in Letra. They weighed approximately one ton and would make half a ton of oatmeal. Such was the demand that the mill had to be booked in advance. The following day, we brought a load of turf that would be used to fuel the fire in the kiln that dried the oats. The ass and cart was used for this purpose.

'My brother John and myself were allowed to go with our father and were excited at the prospect of seeing the mill. We hadn't been so far away from home before and thought the journey would never end. We were fascinated by what we saw there, a great gush of water rushed out a channel and turned a huge wheel.

'As a rule, the miller did not take cash for his services. Instead, he kept a half stone of meal for every hundredweight of meal ground. Local merchants would exchange the meal for cash. By the end of the Second World War, farmers cut back on the amount of oats they sowed as it was no longer profitable – and this marked the decline of the mill.

'Having observed the working of the mill, my brother and I decided to make our own. There was a stream nearby and a dump in a quarry near Glan school contained lots of wheels with cogs. Every Saturday we headed across the Clooncun bog for the dump. This went on for about a month until we thought we had enough material gathered for our experiment. We made a makeshift wheel the size of a dinner plate and set it up in the stream. But the force of the water swept it away, and with it our dreams!'

Corn, on the other hand, was threshed in the fields using a flail, a tool made from two pieces of wood. Martin recalls the arrival of the first threshing machine in Esker village when he was six. 'It arrived in 1926. It was drawn by four donkeys. People used donkeys in preference to horses as they believed that horses would take fright at the sight of the machine. The first threshing machine was old and it broke down regularly. The following year, Pete Keaveny and Johnny Mannion joined up and bought a new machine.'

Flax was grown in the area until the late 1800s, and Martin remembers hearing the stories of scutching the softened plants. 'When the men went card-playing or attended Land League meetings, the women of the village gathered at the house where the scutch was to take place. But scutching wasn't all work for them! They did a bit of matchmaking as well, planning who would make suitable partners. There was a party atmosphere and a singsong. My wife, Sarah Ann, had a towel made from flax grown locally. It is now in the possession of my daughter.'

'How Would You Like To Be Buried with My People?'

'That's my wedding photo,' says Martin, showing me a picture of a happy, glamorous young couple. He met his wife-to-be, Sarah Coyne from Meelick, Glenamaddy, at the local dance hall. He immediately asked her out but says their romance had 'a casual start'. He proposed to Sarah at the dance hall too. 'The whole way of proposing then was to say, "How would you like to be buried with my people?" But I didn't say that. I said, "How about leaving your home tonight?" And she was glad of the chance.'

The couple married in 1947 in St Patrick's Church, Glenamaddy, and they went to Salthill for their honeymoon by hackney car. When they returned, there was little work, so Martin went to England. 'I spent a fortnight walking about from one farm to another, they didn't have work for me and I came upon a neighbour called Michael Comer and he put me to work, and I didn't have any trouble getting work from then on. And I worked for McAlpine on the construction of a big power plant.'

Let There Be Light

Martin is also an inventor. His first invention, in the wake of the Second World War, was a light sensor to encourage hens to produce more eggs. His son, Pat Keaveny, tells the story. 'It was known that artificial light would entice hens to alight from their roosting perches before dawn and induce them to lay before the henhouse door was opened. But as this predated the availability of digital timers, a member of the household had to get up at an unearthly hour to switch on the electric light in the henhouse manually. This proved to be a great inconvenience.'

Martin devised a plan to switch on the light automatically at the desired time using an old-fashioned alarm clock, twine and three inches from a broom handle. He shared his unpatented invention with his grateful neighbours who were also in the business of producing eggs.

'The light would come on at four o'clock in the morning and they laid more eggs,' Martin says. 'One particular neighbour was so pleased that when he died, he gave me seventeen shillings and sixpence, and I bought a suit of clothes with it.'

There was, however, one minor drawback. 'The first night the electricity was turned on, people went to great trouble sweeping the house because they didn't notice the dust before!'

The first night the electricity was
turned on, people went to great
trouble sweeping the house
because they didn't notice
the dust before!'

When the Work Was Done ...

The community in Esker worked together and played together. The village was divided into two by sandhills with six houses on either side, in Baile Nua and Sean Bhaile and there were two visiting houses where people gathered. One of them was the Keaveny household. 'Visiting began when the potatoes were harvested in mid-November and ended in late February when the ploughing started. All under tens were put to bed at six o'clock before the visitors arrived. We resented being put to bed and didn't go to sleep. We knew by the sound of the footsteps who was approaching and we mimicked what they would say before they opened the door. Jimmie Dolan would say, "God bless the work", Patsy Giblin, "God save all here" and Thomas Hussey, "Well, a Mhic". He was known as the 'Mhico'. Some nights they talked about ghosts. Mhico told how he saw a ghost train go through the bog, carriages all lit up, irons clanging on the railway.

> Some nights they talked about ghosts.
> Mhico told how he saw a ghost train
> go through the bog, carriages all lit up,
> irons clanging on the railway.

'We were very noisy upstairs and then a shout would come from below. Things would quieten for a while but soon the *ruaille buaille* would start up again. We were allowed to get up for a while when the visitors left.'

Then in 1938, when Martin was eighteen, his sister Sally brought a radio from England. 'There was a grand programme every week called 'Round the Fire'. Delia Murphy, Éamon Kelly and Sean Ó Síocháin and other good actors and singers took part in it. It was great entertainment for the visitors and not forgetting Lord Haw Haw's broadcasts.

'Billy Martin and his wife were hosts to the visitors in Sean Bhaile. They had a *céad míle fáilte* for everyone. A younger lot of people visited Billy's but seating was a problem. This was overcome by putting a plank from one chair to another and maybe someone would have to sit on a bag of turf. Billy always kept a roaring fire so that everyone was warm. There was card-playing and music. People came from outside townlands to play cards for pigs' heads. Everybody enjoyed a good night's entertainment.'

Martin and Sarah had six children: John lives in the UK while Michael, Pat, Mark, Mary and Martin all live in Ireland. Michael is a retired religious brother and teacher, Pat and Mark are also retired teachers, John is a carpenter, Mary is a retired teacher and accountant, and Martin is a quantity surveyor.

Sarah died at the age of eighty-seven and she is still very much missed. Martin is a religious man and thinks that the afterlife 'might be a better place than the real one'.

Martin died on 3 January 2020, just five months short of his hundredth birthday. May he rest in peace.

Martin Keaveney at Central Park Nursing Home near Ballinasloe, 2019.

1921: Major Events

World

- The USA and Germany sign the Treaty of Berlin, ending the official state of war that still existed between the two countries due to the US Senate's refusal to ratify the Treaty of Versailles

- Adolf Hitler becomes chairman of the Nazi Party in Germany

- Coco Chanel launches her perfume, Chanel No. 5

- On 11 November, the United States buries an unidentified soldier at Arlington National Cemetery in the presence of President Warren G. Harding. The inscription on the tomb reads: 'Here rests in honoured glory an American soldier known but to God.'

- Albert Einstein receives the Nobel Prize for Physics

- David Lloyd George is Prime Minister of the UK

- Charles Bronson, John Glenn and Nancy Reagan are born

Ireland

- Irish War of Independence: The Irish Republican Army occupies and burns the Custom House in Dublin on 25 May; five IRA men are killed and over eighty are captured by the British army

- Captain Con Murphy from Millstreet, County Cork, is executed by British authorities, the first man to be executed in front of a firing squad since the 1916 Rising

- Viscount FitzAlan is appointed Lord Lieutenant of Ireland, the first Roman Catholic since 1685 to hold the position

- James Craig is elected the first Prime Minister of Northern Ireland

- Clashes between Catholics and Protestants in Belfast leave sixteen dead (twenty-three over the next four days)

- Terence MacSwiney's play *The Revolutionist* (set and published in 1914) has its stage premiere at the Abbey Theatre just months after his death

- W.B. Yeats publishes *Michael Robartes and the Dancer* and *Four Plays for Dancers*

- All-Ireland champions: Limerick (hurling) and Dublin (football)

Romance at the Crossroads

Tom O'Mahony
Born 27 February 1921

When we meet, Tom O'Mahony has just celebrated his ninety-eighth birthday with a big family party at his daughter Eileen's home in County Wicklow, where he now lives. 'There were cousins and friends and neighbours,' he tells me as we leaf through the photos of the event, including one of the magnificent red-velvet birthday cake in the shape of Tom's toolbox.

Tom grew up in Ballylanders, seven miles outside Mitchelstown in County Cork – over the Limerick border. He was one of four children of Willie and Nellie (née Quinn).

Tom's earliest memories revolve around the family farm in Ballylanders. Children were given responsibilities from a young age so, from about eight, he found himself helping to milk the cows, clean out the sheds and thresh oats in a barrel. 'It was a very simple life but hard enough.' Families tried to be self-sufficient and Tom's family reared their own pigs as well.

Tom didn't like school. 'It wasn't a terribly good experience and I left at thirteen.' His brother Willie, however, was one of the few at that time who stayed on until Leaving Cert. 'He used to cycle the fifteen-mile round trip to the secondary school in Mitchelstown,' Tom recalls. 'There were twenty-five in the class starting off, but only two stayed the course, and Willie was one of them.'

School Days and Boyhood Mischief

'I went to school in Ballylanders where the community hall now stands,' Tom tells me. 'The boys and girls were in separate rooms back then, and there were just two teachers, one taking the lower classes and the other the more senior ones. I remember my school book cost one penny – and in winter we had to bring in sixpence to cover the cost of fuel.'

There were very few cars on the road in those days, and there were no tarred roads. 'We went to school barefoot in the better weather,' Tom says. 'The roads were very rough, with broken, jagged stones, but somehow we didn't get hurt.'

Tom remembers how they used to play quite a dangerous game on the way home from school. 'We'd often have a stone-throwing match,' he says, 'the old road versus the mountain foot boys. It's amazing no one got seriously injured, looking back on it.'

Tom in the 1940s with a friend, Michael O'Mahony.

On the northern side of Ballymihane Bridge, Tom tells me, a farmer had hammered a sign to a tree overlooking his entrance gate. 'These lands are poisoned', it read. The sign, however, became a target for the stone-throwing boys. 'I was sent by the older boys one day to see if the owner was inside the gate as he was often keeping an eye out. "Are you there, sir?" I shouted. At which point the farmer rushed out and, before I could run, I got a couple of lashes of his whip.'

The sign wasn't the only target for the boys. 'I remember a field of turnips that we raided when we were hungry. We split the turnips on rocks to make them easier to eat.' They also gorged on wild strawberries, which grew across the road. 'They were delicious,' Tom recalls fondly. 'We surely availed of natural food – good healthy fare.'

When Tom left school at thirteen, he went to work on the family farm. 'There was no living to be made there,' he tells me, 'so I asked a man, Dinny Dwyer, for a job and he took me on as an apprentice in his garage.' Tom later moved to the Enniscorthy Motor Company in Wexford, then to Kavanaghs in Fermoy and eventually went back to Ballylanders, where he bought the old barracks in the town for £400.

Romance at the Crossroads

Tom says he literally met his future wife, Alice Martin, at the crossroads. 'Myself and another fella went to a dance, we got our bicycles and we were on the way home together when we came to the crossroads, where we took separate roads. Alice was also coming from the dance. We got talking and I offered to see her home. The next thing it began pouring rain and we ran for shelter under a tree. So we sat on our bicycles till the rain stopped and then I went along the road with her walking her home.'

I was advised not to marry her as she'd know nothing about a garage. "She'll break you up", they told me, "she won't be able to sell petrol, she'll be able to do nothing". But she proved them all wrong, she was able to sell petrol, even bicycles, she could do anything.

But there was a lot of opposition to Tom and Alice getting married. 'I was advised not to marry her as she'd know nothing about a garage. "She'll break you up," they told me, "she won't be able to sell petrol, she'll be able to do nothing." But she proved them all wrong, she was able to sell petrol, even bicycles, she could do anything. Luckily, I didn't listen to any of them. I married her anyway and she opened a lot of their eyes.'

They married the year after they met and

went to Dublin for the honeymoon. They spent a week exploring the city, although Tom notes that Dublin was 'quiet enough then'. The couple had three children – Maura, Billy and Eileen – but Tom claims he never changed a nappy. He took the Pledge when he was twenty-one and is still a Pioneer and proudly wears the Abstinence emblem on his lapel. He has never smoked either.

Today Maura is a midwife, Eileen is the principal in Brittas Bay National School, where she has taught for thirty-eight years, and Billy works for Anglo-Irish Meats.

Explosion

The family settled in the barracks in Ballylanders. It was a big building, three storeys high, and they lived there until 1959 when Tom was seriously injured in an explosion at the garage while he was repairing a car. He was taken by car to the doctor and then to hospital in Limerick where he spent seven months recovering and having several operations and skin grafts. The force of the explosion had blown out the door in the garage.

During this time, Alice ran the business and looked after the family. But Tom couldn't go back to work there and the garage was eventually sold. Today the old barracks houses the local post office.

Tom and Alice made several moves, to a farm in Emly which had a thatched house, to Bansha and finally, to the town of Cahir where they eventually settled.

So what does Tom think of Ireland today? 'People are all trying to "best" one another. When I was young, my father always told us not to do harm to anyone else and to be nice to people.'

Tom is a practising Catholic and recalls how, when he was young, the entire family went off to mass on a Sunday morning on a horse and cart and then returned home to the farm to face their chores.

He believes in an afterlife. 'There must be some place there, there must be a heaven.' And as for death, Tom says it shouldn't bother you. 'As long as you weren't a blackguard – anyone who is good is okay. I do my best.'

And his advice from his long life? 'Do what you have to do, go to mass and say a prayer. And be good to your neighbours.'

A First Election

Anne Blake
Born 11 March 1921

She has minded turkeys, delivered calves and masterminded the Fine Gael camp in the local elections. Ninety-eight-year-old Anne Blake was married to Wicklow county councillor Vincent Blake, who first took his seat in 1976 and who died in 2011. Today their son, Vincent Junior, holds the seat and Anne is still very much a part of the backroom team that keeps the political engine running.

The Blake household was the campaign headquarters. 'I always had a lot of people who were out canvassing coming in to me for their dinners and I was making tea all day. I never went out, though. It was an exciting time for the family but I can tell you about the first time the party wanted him to run. I remember putting out the cows and walking up the road and crying because they wanted him to go for election.'

Their daughter Ettie, the only one of their children to live abroad, came home from Boston each time there was an election. 'My father was a popular man,' Ettie tells me. 'I would go out with him, we would go up all kinds of lanes and open gates and he would always tell me, "You stay there, don't say anything."'

It was an exciting time for the family
but I can tell you about the first
time the party wanted him to run.
I remember putting out the cows
and walking up the road and crying
because they wanted him to go for
election.'

Anne was at the count the first time Vincent was elected. 'In the first election, he got 1,400 first-preference votes. That was exciting because if you got 1,400 number ones, you were getting in. We celebrated. And then the second-last election he went for, he said he was getting too old, it was time to get out, he would have been in his seventies.'

Vincent fought every election from 1978 and remained a councillor until 1998.

The actual polling station back then was the Blake family home in Mullinacuffe. 'It was a great day,' says Ettie. 'Mammy was killed making tea. And Daddy would have us out on the road handing out fliers. And my nan, Henrietta Blake, Daddy's mother, was the polling clerk. She ran the show. It was really a family affair.'

School Memories and a Sporting Romance

Anne Blake was born in Killanure, County Wicklow. Her parents, Jane and Myles Keogh, were farmers, and she remembers their farm and doing a lot of work. 'When we started to milk the cows, that was the hardest.' There were ten children in the family and Anne was the second youngest. 'They're all dead now except for me.'

Anne says school was hard going, they had to walk about two miles each way. 'We went through bogs and fields and up by the old forge. It was a very long journey for little children. There were only two teachers in the school. We brought a lunch of bread and jam, nothing much.'

Anne went on to the convent in Tullow for the remainder of her education and then did a commercial course. 'And then I worked at home until I got married.'

Anne (right) with her sister Molly, taken in the 1940s.

They were a sporting family and Anne was a very good camogie player, playing for Wicklow against Dublin. 'And they beat us as well.'

She met her husband at a football match. 'He was playing along with my brothers. That time, they played in Clonmore, Shillelagh and Ballyconnell. I think he fancied me. We used to meet up at matches and that.' Then when her parents went out in the pony and trap of an evening, Anne and her siblings would have a dance in the house. Vincent would be there because he was friendly with her brothers. 'On one occasion, though, my mother and father came home early and Vincent was mending his bike in the kitchen!'

Eventually, Vincent proposed and they got married. 'It was in the war-time, there were very few weddings back then. We had our reception in Gorey, it was a small hotel. I wore a blue coat, that's all I remember. We didn't go on honeymoon, just back to work the next day, it was tough. Vincent was only four months older than me.'

Anne and Vincent had seven children: Ettie, Tom, John, Marie, Vincent, Sheila and Bernie. John passed away thirty-three years ago. Most of the children were born in Baltinglass Hospital. 'Maternity services back then were bad. I had a little private room but it was a big long corridor of men and women all together. It was tough having babies, there were no drugs, nothing.'

Two of the children were born at home. 'John arrived in the middle of the snow in 1945 and Vincent used to tell the story of how he went to get the nurse in Tinahely but she wasn't there and the doctor wasn't there, so he had to go to Carnew for Nurse Dillon but by the time they got back – John had been born.'

'Years later,' says Ettie, 'Daddy would be telling the story about this, and all the hardship he got the night John was born, and Mammy says to him,

"And what do you think I was doing?" And Daddy says to her, "At least you were in the bed!"'

The War Years

Vincent told his children stories of the Black and Tans coming to his mother's house. His father had died when he was only fourteen. 'His mother lived up there with her two sisters, Kate and Ellen,' says Anne. 'The Black and Tans were demanding money and they had to sell an animal to pay them off.'

Although the family grew a lot of their own produce, Anne says that during the Second World War, times were very hard. 'Everything was rationed. A half ounce of tea and all. We had our own food from the farm though so I suppose we weren't that badly off.'

Farming was much tougher in those years. 'It was all horses,' says Ettie. 'Daddy would be out ploughing with two horses, and we often went up before we went to school to bring him some tea and a sandwich, and he was very proud of his ploughing. It was straight as an arrow and then he would harrow it. He was a very progressive farmer. He sowed corn and beet and wheat.'

Anne was a great seamstress and made beautiful clothes for her children, so they were very proud going to mass. But when they were home from school, they were given their own jobs on the farm. 'I used to send them out to mind the turkeys because the fox might take them or the hawk. The hawk would sweep down. We had about fifty turkeys and Paddy Cassidy would come over and kill them. The children would help to pluck them and wash the crap off their feet and make them look well. Then Vincent would take them to Dublin to the market to sell them.'

> I used to send them out to mind the
> turkeys because the fox might take
> them or the hawk. The hawk would
> sweep down.

'We Are a lot Better Off Today'

Anne is very positive about the state of the nation. 'We are a lot better off today, well off. It's a better place, a lot better. There is still a great sense of community in this area, in Shillelagh, in Mullinacuffe. My neighbours are all very good, and so is my family. I am very close to my family. I have fourteen grandchildren and twenty-three great-grandchildren now. I used to go to the active retirement group, but I am too old now – I am still very independent.'

And as for religion? 'I was brought up in it, afraid of everyone. You had to go to mass and you had to do everything right. I believe in God.'

And does she believe in an afterlife? 'Sometimes, and more times not. At times I wonder is there any next world, when all these things happen, wars and floods, a lot of people killed.' She hopes to meet her husband again and also her son John. 'All my friends are gone. All the people around here. I'm the only one left.'

Anne and her husband Vincent Blake with their grandson John.

Memories of the 1921 Troubles

Patrick Melinn
Born 18 May 1921

Patrick Melinn lives in Retreat Nursing Home in Athlone from where, at ninety-eight, he still has a hands-on approach to Melinn & Sons, the distribution company he founded eighty years ago, as his son calls in regularly to discuss business. 'My son is running it now, here in Athlone. I was very lucky – terribly unlucky and lucky at the same time. I worked as a shop boy, as all lads do, and then I became the manager.'

Patrick was born just outside Athlone to Elizabeth Elliot and Peter Melinn. 'I could write a book about my father, but it wouldn't make sense to you. It would make sense to the locals though. My father died in 1930, he was very young and I was only nine. All our people were involved in the Troubles – 1916 and 1921, all that. I wasn't born then but I heard them talking about it.'

Patrick's father had a small farm outside Athlone. 'He had two brothers and three sisters, and of the two brothers, my uncle Seamus was a rock of sense. Didn't drink or smoke. My father was the same. Years ago, you see, people went to national school and they might get an apprenticeship as a shop boy or a plumber or whatever, there was no money. I served my time way back, and my mother had to give twenty-five pounds for me to spend two years learning a trade. It was grocery.'

Learning the Trade

'That time, everything came in boxes – beans, peas, everything – and you had to put them into pound bags or little cartons. I had a great pair of hands, thank God, and I was a great man to pack stuff. But I was no good at dressing a window. And there were fellas who would dress a window and people would come from miles around to see it.

'What's wrong now, and I hate saying this, the young fella goes to school now and, the next thing, he leaves national school and goes to secondary, and then he comes out and doesn't serve his time doing anything. He goes along and gets a job in the civil service or elsewhere, you know? But he knows nothing. My own family are the same way.

'Whereas I was shown how to bring in a bag of sugar, two hundred weight and before I would bring it in at all, I would have in my mind – I want pounds, two pounds, four pounds, and a few half-stones. The sugar came loose, in a big bag. And we would buy two tonne of sugar at a time. Where I worked, they had a travelling shop, top of the range, they had a big lorry and you would bring a box to the back of the lorry and fill it up. Everything they had in the shop was in that box. The lorry would go every day, they'd have a country run, call to Mrs Jones and roundabouts.'

The young fella goes to school
now and, the next thing, he leaves
national school and goes to
secondary, and then he comes out
and doesn't serve his time doing
anything. He goes along and gets a
job in the civil service or elsewhere,
you know? But he knows nothing.

Patrick bemoans the lack of an account system in the shops now. 'At Christmas, the wife would have maybe fifty turkeys, she paid her bills with that turkey money. Then coming along to the spring, there would be the calves and the sheep and the lambs, and they would be selling the sheep in July and August, and the farmer himself would pay all the big bills like the bag of flour, they all had a system. The farmer could have ten cattle, worth five hundred pounds apiece, but he might not have the paper until he sold them.'

A Foot in Each Camp

Patrick's father Peter and his two brothers were 'Dev's men' during the War of Independence and the Civil War, but his father was also great friends with Michael Collins. 'My father was a commandant in the old Volunteers. He was very popular. Believe it or not, I never saw him with a gun, because he was a promoter for Sinn Féin, and he had a car, though it belonged to the company. He was very popular.

'There were meetings in our house. They would have meetings in different places, his area was Roscommon and Longford and back around to Ballymahon. Now, here is the sad thing about it.

My father was always a sick man. He died in 1930 when he was still young. The thing about it is, even in the split, they were still friends. He was sick for a long time before he died, and he was sick in such a way, the old TB was bad at the time, you could live twenty years with TB but you would be sick.'

The old TB was bad at the time, you could live twenty years with TB but you would be sick.

Gun-Running on Banna Strand

'There was Uncle Seamus, Uncle Joe and my father. They were all very intelligent. They only went to national school but, when they went to Dublin, they educated themselves. At that time, everyone was very religious and they were mass servers and were great with the priests, and the priests would like them because they were pretty intelligent. At that time the movement was beginning to start and they got jobs as shop boys through the IRA.'

Joe got a job in a bacon factory in Tralee, and he got involved with the IRA down there. In fact,

Joe was to be involved in one of the major events of the decade, the gun-running on Banna Strand in 1916. 'Roger Casement, he was bringing in a boatload of guns and they were landed at Banna Strand in Kerry, and Joe could speak a bit of Irish and so could Roger Casement.'

Lieutenant Joseph Melinn's witness statement, given to the Bureau of Military History in December 1948, describes the aftermath of the operation when a number of them were charged with conspiracy to land German arms. The charges against Joe were not proceeded with, but he was deported and ended up in Frongoch Internment Camp in Wales. 'He got jail time in England, the whole bloody lot of them. They were together anyway. He was a character, a great character. They were in jail for a year, or a year and a half, and, when the truce came, they hadn't a bloody penny between them. They were released, no money. They went to the docks and they got a few pound and went and bought a violin, Joe would be able to play anything. And bejesus they got a wad of money from busking. They got home and that was that.'

They went to the docks and they got
a few pound and went and bought
a violin, Joe would be able to play
anything. And bejesus they got a wad
of money from busking. They got
home and that was that.

Standing Up to the Black and Tans

Patrick grew up hearing stories of the Black and
Tans. 'They caused terrible anguish to the people.
They would raid houses and if there was a gun
found that they couldn't account for, they would
take out a young lad and bring him off. My mother
came from about ten miles outside Athlone. When
she used to stay with her parents when my father
was in jail, they would raid that house every night.
They were bastards.

'In Athlone there was a garrison, we had a shop
at the time and there were cousins of ours running
it. There was a lady who used to do the books. The
Black and Tans came in once because my father
had his name over the shop in Irish, Ó Maoilnn.
They had given them notice a few times to take

the name off the door, but they wouldn't. And my father was in jail at that time because he was down in a field and didn't the Black and Tans come down and catch him. He was digging spuds, and they were looking for Peter Melinn and John Elliot, they were big men in the IRA, and they found them and sent them to prison.

'Anyway, this day they came into the shop, in the day time, and the officer in charge was very nice. I remember one time they raided the house at home, and they apologised to my mother. But the Black and Tans would take anything. My grandmother was a great tall, tough woman, and she would stand at the door when they were going out, they'd pick up soap or polish or anything. The best part of it all was, there had to be a captain come along with them, and they would have to bring a peeler along with them as well. So she stood at the door and they were all young lads, and, next thing, she'd find polish and soap in this lad's pocket, and didn't the captain happen to come in the door and say, "What's going on here?" And she says, "I'm searching these lads." And he says to her, "You are perfectly right." It was brilliant.'

Back then, there were settle beds in every house.

'You'd have it there in the kitchen, like a dresser, and at night you would open it up and you would sleep four or five *gasúrs* in it. My mother happened to be there the day they were doing the search of the house. She had lived in that house since she was a child, and she never saw the settle bed opened before, and she had to wait until the Black and Tans arrived to see it opened.'

Patrick also remembers his father-in-law telling him how the Black and Tans burned the whole village of Knockcroghery because of the shooting of a sergeant in the guards in 1921. 'And when the war was over, everyone started looking for compensation. The local parson was a saint. He went up to Dublin and he fought tooth and nail for everyone. I can't remember his name but he was a gentlemen. He was a Protestant, but he gave everything to get compensation for the Catholics. My father-in-law did very well, they gave him compensation and also money for the time his business was closed.'

Pension Principles

'The good part of it is, when the Troubles came to an end, the brothers got jobs. Uncle Joe was in a government job, and they decided to give pensions to them all. But Uncle Joe wouldn't take it. Why? Because it was the Fine Gael government that was in. The laugh of it! My father took it, glad to get it, he'd had a business and it all went bust when the Troubles were on. And when Dev got into power in 1932, he offered him a pension, and he took it, and it wasn't near as good.'

But the Second World War was on the horizon and Patrick says there were shopkeepers who made a fortune on it. 'They were people who had the money. But everything was scarce, we got an ounce of tea, that was nothing. The only thing that was plentiful was bread soda or washing soda.'

> But everything was scarce, we got
> an ounce of tea, that was nothing.
> The only thing that was plentiful was
> bread soda or washing soda.

A Village Romance and Starting His Own Business

'I met my wife down in a little village five miles this side of Roscommon Town. They were in the drapery

Patrick and Mary's wedding,
6 June 1951.

business and, before the war, had had a pipe manufacturer, because Knockcroghery was a noted place for clay pipes. Everyone smoked a clay pipe, there was no such thing as a wooden pipe. There were two or three families making them, and it was a big business.

'There was a dance nearly every Sunday night, and she would go. She was a lovely dancer and she used to dress very well because she had the drapery shop. So I asked her to go to the pictures and that's how it all started. I can't remember asking her to marry me. It was all very simple, I know, because I was a shop boy and I had a bicycle and she had a bicycle and we would go to the pictures. I would have been about twenty-seven or twenty-eight when I got married.

Knockcroghery was a noted place for clay pipes. Everyone smoked a clay pipe, there was no such thing as a wooden pipe.

'At that time, I started my own business – the same business I'm in now, Melinn & Sons. I started in confectionery, minerals and cigarettes. All the big ones, Cadbury, Rowntree's, all that. All the brand names. All the minerals. The amount of minerals, we were buying lorry loads of minerals. Cigarettes and biscuits and chewing gum. Jesus, the amount of chewing gum! It's unnatural. See, now, every young *garsún* has money in his pocket.

'I was very lucky,

Patrick selling from his mobile shop, 1945.

I had two sons. Peter is an accountant and then Brian, since he was very young he was mad for business. I remember when they were going to school, school was only about half a mile up the road, and they would come home for their lunch and Peter would go in, but Brian would come in and ask me what I was working on. He's running it now, he will come into me in the nursing home on the way back every evening and tell me every little bit. Peter is the direct opposite. He'd help you if you wanted to but he thinks we are half mad.'

Patrick also has two daughters: Colette is working in RTÉ and Anne has what her father describes as 'a very nice cushy job' as a lecturer in the University of Limerick.

Counting His Blessings

Patrick considers himself to be a very fortunate man. 'I'm not sick. I'm here, I have my bungalow down the road and we got into a great business. I'm no saint, but I do everything that I should do. I met a lot of people in hard times. If they owed me money, I would say, "Take your time." And if there was a fella or woman going to mass with a big rosary beads or a missal ... now, I'll say no more!'

He says he is not religious. 'But I am better than a religious person, I think. I was brought up as a Catholic, did all the things you should do as a Catholic and still do. But I think, as a Catholic, that the Church have only themselves to blame. They got so strong, they were dictating to us, and I didn't like that. I go with the flow.'

He believes in God. 'But I get confused sometimes. I said to myself, *Where are all the people who have died? Where did they go? Heaven is such a big place, how are we all going to get a bite to eat?* But maybe you won't want to eat when you're dead. It's very hard to know. All the people that have died that belonged to me, none of them have ever come back to say it's a great place. You'd be baffled.'

A Rambling House

Kevin Kealy
Born 20 June 1921
Sr Máire Kealy
Born 4 September 1926

Kevin Kealy is one of the country's best-known veterinary surgeons, but he almost became a priest, only just stopping short of his ordination.

He has also been Lord Mayor of Dundrum in County Dublin, but he started life on a small farm in County Laois. 'My grandfather was a well-known person in the area, he was a rate collector. He was also involved in the Land League.' Kevin's father was William Patrick Kealy and his mother was Mary Martha Forde. William had been born into a forty-acre farm but there were seven children and, like all small farmers, the farm could only go to the eldest, who was Kevin's uncle, so the rest had to go out and work. William did a correspondence course in accounting 'with some crowd in England'.

'In those days there was a very active coal-mining industry in the area around Wolf Hill owned by a very famous horse trainer, Senator J.J. Parkinson.' This is where William got his first job. Parkinson was a vet as well and lived in a place called Maddenstown Lodge on the Curragh.

Being Put to Work Early

One of Kevin's earliest memories is of feeding calves when he was four or five, and he says he was put to milking at an early age. His aunt Rose used to rear turkeys and he would feed them and help with the pigs and the hay-making in the summer. Then, when he was about nine, he remembers going to the fair in Athy. 'It was like a dung heap on a Fair Day, cattle all over the street.

'I have very vivid memories of my youth. Forty acres wasn't a great swathe of land to rear a big

Kevin Kealy's earliest photo, as a toddler in 1923.

family on, so as soon as my uncles and aunts got to an age, they moved, you know. The eldest was John, then my uncle Stephen who was a Christian Brother, he was a superior in Kells at one time, and a superior in Doon in Limerick when he died. And then Malachy, who was a garda sergeant in Dundrum in Dublin, and my aunt Mary, who did nursing in England but came home and married a farmer who lived about four or five miles from where we were reared. Next came my father and Rose and then Tim, who emigrated to America. Uncle John inherited the farm, he was a bachelor all his life. He was like all those bachelors in the country who get to fifty and think of getting a young wife.'

But he never found one. 'Any ones he had his eye on, they wouldn't have an interest in a fifty-year-old with a poor farm. I remember they'd all be making fun, having a bit of craic about the fact he wasn't married and all that. I remember one day when I was in my early teens, we used to retreat to Wolf Hill during holiday time. He came into the kitchen and the eyes were dancing in his head and he says, "Do you remember they were talking to me about such and such a lassie? Well, she's fallen

The Kealy family home in Prosperous, Co Kildare.

and broken her leg. What would I be doing with a woman sitting in a chair with her leg up in a plaster?" He was found dead in a ditch, poor fella, only in his fifties when he died.'

A Rambling House

Kevin says there wasn't much in the way of entertainment when he was young. 'Ours was a rambling house. People dropped in every night of the week, there would be someone sitting around the fire, drinking tea, telling stories. You have to remember in those days there was no telephone, no radios, no telly. No nothing, as they used to say. But we were as happy as Larry.

'I can remember the people who used to call to the house at night. There was a fella called Jim McGrath, they lived across the field from us so he was a regular rambler in our house. There was a fella called Fleming whose brother was a superintendent in the guards in Dublin in the 1930s. He was in charge of the traffic in the city. Tommy Brennan was another one, he lived a few fields over from us, they used to call him the bog lark. They'd tell stories, there would be a bit of craic, local gossip mainly, and maybe once a week the paper would be got. None of them were boozers. They'd have a cup of tea. They'd head home about half nine or ten o'clock. We'd be going off to bed at that time because, of course, there was no electricity either.'

Ours was a rambling house. People dropped in every night of the week, there would be someone sitting around the fire, drinking tea, telling stories. You have to remember in those days there was no telephone, no radios, no telly. No nothing, as they used to say. But we were as happy as Larry.

And living without electricity was normal at that time. 'My aunt Rose did all the cooking, we had an open fire with a crane and she would hang the pots on that. She had a skillet which she used to bake the cakes and bread and we used to make our own butter. It was melt-in-your-mouth stuff.'

So what was on the menu? 'We'd have bacon, very rarely would we see steak. There were no butchers in the area. We grew our own vegetables and we used to sell our butter. There was a fella called Con Dennehy, he used to come from Cork and buy the butter. He used to operate as a shop on top of Wolf Hill in the Slieve Blooms. He would set up a stall and buy butter from us and all the people around, he was known as the 'butter man'. But Dennehy was murdered one day in 1938. He was shot dead on the road between a place called the Swan and Fairymount, robbery being the probable motive. He used to travel that road once a week going up to Smiths to buy butter.'

In 2006, TG4 produced a documentary on the murder in their *Ceart Agus Coir* series that looked at the history of the death penalty in Ireland. The man convicted of Dennehy's murder, James Dermot Smyth, was executed at Mountjoy prison on 7 January 1939.

A School Boycott and a Miners' Strike

Kevin loves the story of how his father and mother met. 'There was a school in Wolf Hill and it was like a lot of the schools in those days, the master taught the boys and there was a woman teacher upstairs for the girls. But this lady that was teaching upstairs, her husband bought a farm from which the tenants had been evicted, and the neighbourhood took a very poor view of that. The farmers all got together and decided that they would boycott the school and wouldn't send the children there.

There was a fella called Billy Bolton, he was one of the small farmers, and he went down to Stradbally where there was a Captain Cosby, the Cosbys are still in Stradbally I think. He bought some kind of a carriage that could be drawn by horses, and he provided a transport service for the children. They'd all accumulate at the top of Wolf Hill and he would pick them up and drive them to a place called Bán Óg. This was before I was born, this was probably 1913. So there was a big dispute going on for a long time and eventually some kind of mediation was set up. They decided that if the lady resigned out of the school and someone else

Kevin's class in O'Connell's School. Kevin is first on
the left, 2nd row.

was brought in as a teacher, they would abandon
the boycott.'

The teacher resigned and was replaced by
Kathleen Forde (Kevin's aunt) from Galway but,
after a few years, she decided to become a nun.
Then another sister, Delia, was appointed, but
she also became a nun. 'Next, the third sister, my
mother, became the replacement teacher. Then my
father and mother had a romance between them
and they got married in 1920 and I was born in
1921.' With both his parents working, Kevin says
he was mainly reared in his paternal grandmother's

house which was just down the road from their house. Her name was Maggie Dunne.

When Kevin was about three, there was trouble in the mines. 'There was a strike of the workers for a start and then water got into the mines and as a result of it, about 1926 the whole thing was closed down. But my father had made a good impression on the owner, Parkinson, and he brought my father to Newbridge and installed him there as an auctioneer for a few years. So that meant my mother, who was teaching in Wolf Hill, had to find a job down that part of the country and she got a job in Prosperous in 1926.'

Máire's School Memories

Kevin's sister Máire, being five years younger, went to school in Prosperous where her mother taught. 'There was a girls' school and a boys' school,' she remembers, 'and my mother taught in the boys' school, which was on the ground floor. The girls' school was on the first floor. There were two teachers upstairs teaching the girls. I have a vague memory of walking up the stairs and shouting, "I'm coming." She liked living in Prosperous but recalls how 'the boys used to gallop up and down with me in some kind of a go-cart and I remember the neighbour shouting, "You'll kill the child."

'We all went to live in Dublin then and I went to Iona Road Holy Faith, a very good school. But I was very subject to colds and coughs and bronchitis and all sorts, and evidently I was very often absent from school. I remember Sr Mobhi taught me. She was very nice and used to let us go for a little sleep. I have only good memories of that. I also remember writing on a slate.

When she was in Junior Infants in Dublin, the school sent for Máire's father to complain that she was absent too often and was bringing down the average number on the rolls, which would eventually affect their teaching staff. So she had either to come to school or leave and move elsewhere. At their suggestion, she was moved to the private school in Holy Faith Glasnevin.

'My mother was still teaching in Prosperous, she stayed there all her life teaching. She stayed there during the week and came back at weekends. I suppose she had to because there were four children to bring up.'

Leaving Behind the Dublin Smog

Máire and her brother, Stephen, both got pneumonia. 'That was 1932 because the Eucharistic Congress was on. Stephen was in my father and mother's bedroom and I was in another one, and the doctor used to come, and do you know what they used to put on your chest in those days? A thing called 'antiphlogistine', it was a heated red flannel with some medication on it, it would soften the cough. Anyway, as a result of being so ill, the doctor said they should send me back to the country for a while, I seemingly wasn't thriving in the Dublin city air.

'So I went down to my great aunt in Graignahown. My father's sister, Mary, was married to a man called John Brennan. She was his second wife, and his own family were now grown up, and Aunt Mary took me to live with them for two or three years in the countryside. I absolutely loved it and I loved my aunt Mary. She was a more affectionate person than my mother. My mother would be a bit standoffish. I don't want to be denigrating my poor mother but she was a different character. My aunt was very motherly with me, and I made my First Communion while I was down there.'

Back to Dublin and Trouble with the Inter

Máire was then sent to the Dominican Scoil Chaitríona in Eccles Street, Dublin, where everything was *as Gaeilge*. 'I thought they were lovely people. I was very happy and we liked the nuns, they were very friendly and would talk to us. The principal in 1928 was Mháithir Treasa Ní Fhlanagáin, a wonderful person. She wanted us to speak Irish all day long but, of course, being children we lapsed into English now and again. She never gave out but she would say, "*Gaeilge anseo mais led do thoil é*", or "*Ah, cailíní ... Gaeilge.*" '

Sr Máire Kealy just before she joined the Dominicans in September 1945.

But Marie was about to face the trauma of failing the Intermediate Certificate examination. 'Somebody once said to me, "I thought it was impossible to fail the

Inter", and I replied, "Well, I managed it!" Because I was running around. Well, I roared crying, bawled my eyes out. I cried all the way home. But I was to be surprised by my mother's reaction. I thought she would give out to me, I thought it would be terrible, and thought my father wouldn't be pleased either. She opened the door and I fell in crying, "I failed the Inter." But she said, "Come in, that's not the end of the world, come on in."

'And I didn't hear another word about it for two weeks, and then they said, "Máire, we've organised that you're going to go in as a boarder into Eccles Street, we haven't been fair to you." Now at this time, the three boys had gone off to Kilkenny, to the boarding school. I was in the house alone, my mother was down in Prosperous, my father was out working, we had a housekeeper and she was the only one that saw me. So I would come home and throw my bag in the door and go out and play skipping or whatever was going on out in the road at the time. Becoming a boarder was the best thing that ever happened me, because from then on I never failed an exam.'

'He Was Born Delicate'

There were five children in the Kealy family but the youngest, Liam, died as a child. 'As they used to say in the country,' says Kevin, 'he was born delicate. I don't know what it was he had but he died about seven years of age. I often speculated that he might have had cerebral palsy or something like that because he never got out of the pram, you know, and we were isolated out there on a small farm in the country. My aunt Rose really nursed him. He's buried in Wolf Hill.'

Máire, now Sr Máire, remembers Liam too. 'I was three years older than Liam Patrick, and I have a vague notion of standing at the wall in the living room in Prosperous, looking at my mother with this baby in her arms. He was born in August 1929. The medics at the time said he might live seven years, and he died between his sixth and seventh birthday. It must have been very hard; I was conscious of his death. My father's mother took him over and kept him down in Wolf Hill, where they came from. She died a year before he did. Aunt Rose minded Liam until he died.'

A Well-Travelled Priest, and His Brother Who Chose To Be A Vet

Kevin was the eldest in the family. His brother Brendan also went on to become a veterinary surgeon and Stephen joined the Columban Fathers in Dalgan Park in Navan. 'He was posted to the Philippines and was several years there, then he got some sort of a lung infection and they brought him home. And they sent him to King's Lynn in Norfolk for a few years

Kevin receives a blessing from his brother, Rev Stephen Kealy, following his ordination, December 1949.

to recover his strength. When he was duly recovered, they sent him to Lima in Peru and then to Arizona because he was a fluent Spanish speaker. He was in a Spanish parish outside Phoenix for about fourteen or fifteen years. Then he was posted to Hollywood, of all places. He was there for a couple of years and then eventually they retired him to a place called Bristol just outside Boston and then he retired to Dalgan and he died there.'

Kevin did his Leaving Certificate at St Kieran's College in Kilkenny and then he entered the seminary, where he remained for six years before leaving just a couple of months before he was due to be ordained. So why did he leave? 'Ah, it's a complicated story. St Kieran's was a seminary for secular priests and, of course, in those days the Church was overcrowded with candidates for the priesthood. Nine or ten of us joined up from my Leaving Cert class. I left in 1945 and I went into the veterinary college in UCD.'

Joining the Dominicans – A Spur-of-the-Moment Decision

Máire also had a vocation and joined the Dominican sisters. She is now retired and living in

Sr Máire Kealy in
Postulant's dress,
Dominican Novitiate,
Kerdiffstown, Naas, 1945.

the convent in Sion Hill in Dublin. She joined the order straight from school. 'I went down to the novitiate in Kerdiffstown, County Kildare. But it was a spur-of-the-moment decision. I left school in June, after the exams, and, during the summer holidays, I had a friend called Sarah Walsh. She was from Wicklow and lived near Glendalough. I had a letter from Sarah saying, "I'm going to Kerdiffstown, will you come?"

'My mother was delighted that I would be a nun, whereas my father, he was very silent about it. He didn't say much, just, "If you're sure that's what you want." Kevin had just left the priesthood at that stage and he was the only one who told me to think hard because he had realised that he had made a big mistake, the priesthood wasn't for him at all. But I said, "Of course I know what I'm doing."'

And just like Kevin's class, several of Máire's year joined religious orders. 'Sarah Walsh came, Mary Murphy came, I was there, that was three out of Scoil Chaitríona, and there were maybe three or four more from the Dominican College and there was a crowd that came from Cabra and Sion Hill.'

The novitiate in Kerdiffstown was very strict, postulants' letters were read coming and going. 'You couldn't get home, and you knew you would never get home in the Dominican setup at the time. You entered and you entered for life. I was nineteen when I went in and I was just bordering twenty-one when I was professed.'

You couldn't get home, and you knew
you would never get home in the
Dominican setup at the time. You
entered and you entered for life.

Máire remembers her profession as a very formal affair. 'It was August. After one year, you were received and you got the habit. That was a big thing, to get the habit.' The postulants were dressed as brides for the ceremony. 'There were clothes upstairs, old wedding dresses or whatever they were that had been donated to the convent. They were washed every year and put away and then brought out the next year, and that went on for twenty years. They weren't fashionable but they were white and long and you had a veil on you. You wouldn't be delighted to be walking around in these things. We used to be laughing about it, the shoes and stuff, they were ludicrous. They were 1920s and we were 1940s girls.

'You got a white veil for one year and then the black veil. You were two years professed before you left the novitiate. When I was received, we were given religious names and I was given the name Cynthia. The name comes from St Hyacinth, the patron saint of Poland.'

Photographs were not permitted at the profession and the only visitors allowed were parents, although others could come along in the afternoon.

Becoming a Teacher – and an Author

Máire went sent back to Eccles Street. 'Yes, much to my delight, because they had decided that I would be trained for primary teaching. There were two of us from our set, Chrissy Lawlor and me, who were assigned to study for entry to Carysfort.'

After she qualified, Máire's first job was teaching in Cabra. 'There were about fifty-six of them, that's the number that used to be in the class. Some of them keep up with me still.' And those same past pupils even organised an evening out for her many years later.

Sr Máire is an accomplished historian and author and has penned two books on the history of the Dominican order in Ireland, *Dominican Education in Ireland, 1820–1930*, which was her PhD thesis at Lancaster University, and *From Channel Row to Cabra*. 'Channel Row is North Brunswick Street today. The Channel was a river, it meant the road beside the river. When they came up from Galway in 1717, the nuns settled in Channel Row and they were there until 1919 or whatever. Then they went to Clontarf, and it was disastrous, it wasn't a success for them at all and their numbers went down.'

Graduation, Lectureship and the Eucharistic Congress

Kevin graduated from UCD in 1950 – he got first place in his class and went on to win a number of other awards over the years. His brother Brendan was already practising as a vet in Ardee and asked Kevin to join him. 'And I thought, why not?'

One of Kevin's strongest memories of the years he spent working on farms as a vet was 'the plague of flies on the farms in those days, there were dung heaps in the yard or the haggard and every kitchen had yellow fly paper. We used to pull bushy branches and attach them to the horses' heads when they'd be ploughing in the fields to keep the flies off them!

'The lectureship in veterinary surgery at UCD then became vacant so the college got in touch and asked would I apply for it, and I did. But I was only a year and a half qualified at the time, and I didn't get it. A year later it came up again, and they asked me again would I go for it. I said no this time because I was doing well for myself. Money in my pocket and the only practice in town. So they held interviews but didn't appoint anybody. And then, five years later, they put it up again and I went for it this time and I got it. I went to teach surgery there in the veterinary college to final-year students.'

Kevin has strong memories of
the Eucharistic Congress which
took place in Dublin in June 1932.
Dublin was chosen as it was also the
1,500th anniversary of St Patrick's
arrival in Ireland. After the final mass
in the Phoenix Park, around half a
million people gathered on O'Connell
Bridge for a blessing.

Kevin has strong memories of the Eucharistic Congress which took place in Dublin in June 1932. Dublin was chosen as it was also the 1,500th anniversary of St Patrick's arrival in Ireland. After the final mass in the Phoenix Park, around half a million people gathered on O'Connell Bridge for a blessing. 'I noticed Dev at the Eucharistic Congress. I always voted. My mother was always a strong Fianna Fáil supporter until Dev vetoed a rise for the teachers, after which she voted Fine Gael instead. I usually voted Fianna Fáil. My father was a secretary of the Kildare Fine Gael cumann although I think he voted for Dev in later years. I never got involved in politics, except in veterinary politics.

Falling for the Older Man

And so we move on to love and romance and Kevin's wife, Joan, joins us to make sure we get it right and to point out that she is fifteen years younger than her husband! 'Well, I knew Kevin, I was about fourteen and I brought his dog to a show in the RDS on St Patrick's Day. It was a wheaten terrier, a lovely dog. Unfortunately he had a cut on one of his legs, and Kevin never told me and sent me off to parade this dog around. The dog did not win. But I had memories of Kevin before that because his parents used to play poker with my parents and he used to drop in late at night and my mother would give him a jar of whiskey. In those days, you could drive after having a drink.

'Then I met him at a hop. He used to play the piano. And I saw him at this dance, some sort of a charity run by an aunt of mine. He was going off on holidays to America at this stage and he said, "We'll go out when I come back." I was delighted to have a date. That was October, we were engaged at Christmas and married in April.

'I'll never forget the wedding day. We were married at nine o'clock in Booterstown, it lashed out of the heavens, I was all in white. The organist was a lady who played appalling stuff but she was my friend, so we put up with it. Afterwards, we went to the Hermitage Golf Club because, at that stage, it was too late to book a hotel. I think we had chicken and ham and trifle and coffee. And then we went to Majorca the same day and on the way back we had a few nights in London and he went to a conference. I was only a child, really, I was twenty-four, and not a grown-up twenty-four. And then, in the next ten years, I had six children.'

The age difference was initially a bit of a shock for Joan's parents. 'But they knew him already. They were quite agreeable to it really because they thought he would be a steady person for me – I was a flippety gibbet. We were happy but we had to get a dispensation because we were second cousins.'

The couple were very compatible, as Joan loves animals too. 'It just seemed the right thing. Then Kevin tried to make me do the Benevolence Society but I was a total failure and that was quickly taken out of my hands and he did it for me. I was so lacking in maturity. I was used to my mother being at home doing the cooking and I fell into that pattern for a couple of years, as a wife, and I didn't even have ideas about going back to work. What started me thinking about it was when my mother died and I had six children all around and I kept lifting up coffee cups that were scattered everywhere and I thought, *This can't be it*. So I became a physiotherapist and worked in St James's. I am retired now.'

Lord Mayor of Dundrum and the Tour de France

When the couple moved to Dundrum in County Dublin, Kevin became very involved in the Dundrum Residents' Association and he was elected Lord Mayor of Dundrum in 1997, the year before they brought the prestigious Tour de France through the village. But because they were busy resurfacing the roads for the race, they didn't have time to elect a mayor, so Kevin got a two-year stint.

A Pioneer in Radiology

Kevin tells me about the time his professor at the vetinerary college on Shelbourne Road, Prof. McGeady, a Donegal man, asked him if he would

Kevin with his father and mother on his
graduation day, 1950.

have any interest in an old x-ray machine that
was lying around. 'I said I would, though I didn't
know anything about x-ray machines. I was in the
Department of Agriculture at the time and I looked
up various things in a reference book. And I saw
that there was an advisor to the government there,
Reynolds was his name, in radiology, so I rang
him up and we arranged to meet. I told him about
this mission I had to get interested in radiology,
and I asked him did he have any ideas. "The
human radiologists have a group here that meet

every month," he told me, and said that I should meet them. At that time there were a number of American foundations and institutions helping out Irish colleges, and all around Europe. One of them was the Kellogg Foundation, so on the advice of the powers that be in UCD, I applied for one of these fellowships and I got it, to go to Philadelphia and study radiology.'

Kevin spent fourteen months in Philadelphia studying radiology with human doctors. 'They had no school for vets,' he tells me. Then he got involved with two vets from Glasgow and Cambridge and they set up the British Institution of Radiology. Kevin was the chairman in 1964. 'I went on a tour of Europe looking at x-ray machines and seeing what we were going to buy. The annual meeting of 1968 was due to be held in Dublin because I was the chairman, so I wrote to the guys in America to see would they come. We had a big crowd from abroad, and we founded the International Foundation of Radiology and the first conference was here in Dublin. They all panicked when they found out these guys were descending on the city.'

Kevin retired in 1988 when his eyesight deteriorated. 'I had to give up driving and I can't read the paper anymore, even with the glasses. I used to play the organ at mass on a Sunday but I don't do it anymore because I can't read the music.' But Kevin had to accept mandatory retirement anyway, aged sixty-seven. He says retirement should be up to the individual. 'Some people want to retire, I didn't want to retire. If I was seventy now I would fight it.' After his official retirement, he travelled abroad, lecturing in veterinary radiology.

In 1979, Kevin wrote *Diagnostic Radiology and Ultrasonography of the Dog and Cat*, which proved to be a bestseller in the veterinary world. He has revised it a number of times and it is still the standard text today, translated into nine languages, including Japanese and Chinese.

Bringing German to the Seminary

He also speaks fluent German (or '*ein wenig*' [a little], as he protests), which he learned as the Second World War was breaking out. It was during his first year in the seminary. 'I could hear all these radio stations so I got the scrambler and I learned it literally. And then I thought, what could I do to progress it? We got holidays at Christmas so I went home and looked up the address of the German embassy, it was on Northumberland Road then. So I went down there and told them that I would like to learn German, and they said they would make me a member of their library.

'Discipline in the seminary was so strict, it was there I expected trouble. I told the seminary what I was up to. The embassy was supposed to post me books. But anyway, I plugged away and I got better at it. I used to do a few German songs, learn them off by heart, give me a bit of vocabulary. I was interested in German since then. I even at one stage gave a lecture in German, at the University of Berlin. They said I had a country accent and I got a letter afterwards saying that the students said I had a Bavarian accent.'

An Air-Raid Shelter in the Backyard

Máire remembers the 'stop press' editions of the newspapers announcing that war had broken out in 1939. 'People came out and bought the paper and found out the world was at war. There were no radio news programmes then, certainly not television. There would have been radios but, in the middle of the day, it didn't work. I wasn't frightened, I remember thinking war would be a really interesting thing to happen. That shows you what sense I had, I was twelve or thirteen then.'

But Máire's father wasn't taking any chances

and he built an air-raid shelter in the backyard. 'It was reinforced concrete, not underground, but dug down a bit. My father went up and planted lettuces on top of it. We were in it the night the North Strand was bombed. I remember that. Kevin and Stephen were in boarding school, Brendan was probably in first year in college so we were the only two children at home. It was a Friday night when we heard the bombs, we could hear aircraft flying overhead.

'The state had a whole setup and called someone the Air Raid Precaution Person. You could volunteer to be one and, when the air raids came out, you had to go and rescue people. That night there were whistles and all hell broke loose. We weren't terribly far from the Mater and the ambulances were flying up from the North Strand. We were very close to it as the crow flies. So we didn't go into the air-raid shelter that night but we went in the next night because we heard an aeroplane, and we sat and shivered, we had nothing to sit on. There was no furniture. We sat in it for about ten minutes and we were perished with the cold and we came in. It was never used again.'

When their parents died Kevin inherited the

house and he put it up for sale. When it was sold a second time 'myself and Kevin said we would go down and say we were interested in buying it. We went through to the yard and weren't there two fellas up trying to knock the air-raid shelter down. We said, "We remember that going up", and they were roaring laughing and said, "Well, it is hard enough to bring down anyway."'

The war years weren't too hard for the Kealys. 'We managed all right. We had Auntie Mary down in Graignahown sending us up butter and things that were rationed in Dublin. We were never short, we got enough.'

Looking Back – and Forward

Sr Máire is very unhappy with the state of Ireland today. 'I think they lack leadership – strong, intelligent leadership. Look at these people who are living in one room of a hotel and have to get out tomorrow and bring all their children – that is wrong! Get the people who have no houses, get them decent living accommodation and try to build up the state again.'

She always votes in elections and referendums. 'I voted for divorce but out of conscience I voted against same-sex marriage, but sure if people want to do what they want to do, they're going to do it anyway, whether it is the law or not.'

The role of women has always interested her. 'My mother was a teacher and she didn't like de Valera because he decided that married women shouldn't be teaching. Anyone who was trained before that could stay on, and that's how she kept her job. But anyone who got married after that had to leave and get a job elsewhere. The civil service was the same. It's good that women can work, but I do think there is an awful strain on families trying to cope with all that and bring up the children, and I am sorry that children have to go into crèches and nursery schools or whatever.'

And what about the decline of vocations? What about the future of nuns? 'Well, if you could answer that now you might get a bonus from all the nuns in the country. I don't know. Maybe our day is done.'

Kevin says he is happy with his life. 'I've enjoyed life, by and large. I never had any serious troubles apart from medical ones, COPD. But I am alive. I think there's a certain amount of luck in how a person's career goes. A good amount relies on the circumstances that you find yourself in and how you handle them. It's very hard to say how you would operate in certain circumstances. I never thought I would get the chance to go to America, but when we got the chance, we went.'

A Philosophical Take on the Afterlife

Máire tells me that she feels very uneasy about death. 'The doctor said I have eleven more years and I said, "Oh God, I don't want to live another eleven years." And he said, "Ah we will take one off and leave you with ten." But I'm very lonely. All my companions, my age group, are going, going. Sr Louis Dominic died in May this year and now Sr Isabelle in Galway and myself are the only two left of the set that entered in 1945.'

> The doctor said I have eleven more years and I said, 'Oh God, I don't want to live another eleven years.'

She believes in an afterlife. 'Well, having spent my life living in the hope of an afterlife, living and working because I believe there is a God and I believe in Jesus, the thing to do was to help other people learn the same thing and help them on the way. I'm over seventy years a nun. I don't think that's all gone down the swanny and that there's nothing after when you go down in the ground. I don't.'

But how do we know what it is? 'We don't know. That's where the faith is, you hang on in there. Death is the end of life, that's for sure. That's what it is all about, that your life is ended. But my problem is, afterwards. Think of all the people that have gone. To think of it in terms of the whole cosmos, there must have been some creative mind somewhere, whatever shape it takes, to organise the cosmos as it is and as it developed down the centuries, more centuries than we admit. Because we talk about the twenty-first century but sure there were hundreds of centuries before that.'

Catching Roses

Anne Kennedy
Born 3 December 1921

'I was born under the crown!' That was the boast of Frank Kennedy, Anne's husband. 'He was a lot older than me and it was only years afterwards that I thought, *Sure so was I, because the Anglo-Irish Treaty was signed just three days after I was born!*'

Anne entered this world in Holles Street Hospital in Dublin, her mother was from Dundrum in Dublin and her father from Abbeyleix in County Laois. The first thing she tells me is a story about her brother Jack, who once asked her mother, 'Where did you meet my father?' And she said, 'I was walking down the footpath and he came up opposite and wouldn't let me pass!' And that's how they met.

'I was walking down the footpath and
he came up opposite and wouldn't
let me pass!' And that's how
they met.

Anne had seven older brothers, one of them had had a twin sister but sadly, she died in 1918 in the big flu. 'Willie was the eldest, Jimmy, Jack, Paddy, Bob, Joe and Eoin. And then me. And there was about a year and a half or two years between each of them.

The family lived at number 266 in Windy Arbour, Dundrum, that was the number of the house at the time. 'It's twenty-two now! The numbers have all changed.'

Earliest Memories, Childhood Games

Anne says her earliest memory was of 'sleeping in the bed with my mother and father, at the top of the bed. And then there was one stage that my brother Unie [Eoin's pet name], was at the bottom and I remember him saying to me, won't you mind my feet? And that didn't last long and I went into a cot. A rocker cot, one of the big ones. One of the lads used to come in and stay in the room because

Anne with brothers Eoin and Paddy, 1932.

I was afraid of the dog. We had only gas light then. And then when he'd be sneaking out the door, I'd say, "I'm not asleep!"'

Anne was particularly fond of her brother Jack, the third eldest, who was born without fingers on one hand. 'He told me afterwards that my mother told him his baby hand had got caught in the womb. It was very sad for Jack because he dropped out of school because of the hassle he was getting and, in later years, told me that our mother should have insisted he stay in school. He had that little thing, that he missed out on school. You could say he was illiterate. But not with money, just writing. He used to say, "Teach me how to spell words," and I did, as a kid. Spelled out the words for him.'

When Anne was a child, Dundrum was in the countryside, there were fields everywhere and that was where the children played, everything from chasing to creating their own little games.

'When I was about seven we had one play with the Webster girls who lived next door, there were about four of us. It must have been Snow White and I was the mirror! My friend May Tobin would say, "Mirror, mirror on the wall, who's the fairest of them all?" And she'd answer, "You, my queen, are the fairest of them all", or something like that, but then there's one part where it goes, "Get down, she cried, and pick me some blossoms", and May called out, "Get down, she cried, and pick me some bosoms!" And of course we all started laughing and May ran off crying. The plays were great that we made. There were big gardens, with pigsties at the end. They were never used for pigs.

'There was skipping and kicking the polish tin. And making beds with the chalk and then Relievio. And then we went over to the fields a lot, every day in the summer, picking the daisies and making daisy chains. We were never idle, I know that much.

'We used to climb trees and we made up this language, this is the truth. I remember one of them was "a scum a scum a sco" and that was supposed to mean something, and then the girls would answer with a different one – and then one of them started to cry when I said a different one again. She said I was laughing at her and she went crying to her mother and she didn't come back out.'

Following the Star

Anne remembers her first day at school when her brother Unie was given the task of delivering her. 'It was St Anne's in Milltown, where the film star Maureen O'Hara [FitzSimons] went.' Maureen's sister Florrie FitzSimons was in Anne's class, Maureen was two classes ahead of her and then there was Peggy who entered the convent in Milltown and became a nun. There was also another sister, Margot, and two boys.

'Maureen spoke about it afterwards, she said something about the school but, you see, she couldn't say much because her sister was a nun.

'I hated the nuns. There was a Sr Perpetua. I didn't like her. You could hear her coming along with the keys rattling. She pulled me up one day, I was coming down the spiral staircase: "Annie Mulhall, I want to speak to you! Why don't you go home and tell your mother she will have to make your gymslip longer, it's too short. Tell your mother I want to see her." My mother went down and she said, "Annie is my only girl and she doesn't have anyone to hand the clothes down to and she will wear them." My mother used to make gymslips and everything, she was great before she suffered a bad fall. The fall kind of knocked her.

'I remember a lot about my schooldays. Miss O'Meara was the Irish teacher. We had these little badges: "*Labhair Gaeilge Linn.*" She insisted that we speak Irish and we did. We spoke a lot of Irish there. Now, I must say, the teachers were lovely, we had Mr Goddard for drill class [a form of PE]. I loved that class. We had the dumbbells, the barbells, all that and we had a big tableau at the end of the school year out in the grounds. I loved it. The figure marching! I used to love doing it.'

As the only girl, Anne was her father's pet. 'My mother was kind of cold. She loved the boys. She loved Unie, he was the boy who had lost the twin. And although she got me everything I needed, there was no kissing or anything. It was the same everywhere, there was no having a hug or anything. But my dad did show affection.'

A Farm in Dundrum – and Mother's Early Death

Anne's dad was a farm labourer in Mellon's of Dundrum. 'They had a big farm, and my father worked there and used to take me up to the farm every Sunday. Then he'd be doing something with the cows and he'd leave me. There was an old man that used to be there and he had a beard and he gave me a piece of cut glass that was all colours – broken glass – and I had that for years. You'd twist it and see all the blues and yellows, I'll never forget that.

Anne and her dad, 1934.

'We had a great butcher's shop in Dundrum, Horlicks, my mother used to send me up and I would get pork, big lumps of meat, chops. It was all written down for me on a list.

'My father used to take me on the crossbar of his bike. He'd put a cushion on the crossbar and cycle out to Merrion Strand. I must have been about three or four at that time. And I remember going out and we would pick cockles, my mother loved cockles, and we would bring them home. I would carry the bag while he would cycle the bike. I wouldn't eat them, it seemed my mother loved them. She was the only one who would eat them.'

My father used to take me on the crossbar of his bike. He'd put a cushion on the crossbar and cycle out to Merrion Strand.

Anne herself was picky about her food. 'I know I was picky. I *loved* my porridge, I loved the milk going around the edge of the porridge. My mother was a great cook. My brother Jack helped, he reared me. And he told me once that when he used to carry me, I used to put my hand down and feel for his hand. He told me this years and years later. But Jack was so good, he was never appreciated but he made a good life. He got married, got a job in PYE, which made televisions, and then he went to England and worked there and then came home to Ireland, and his wife Beth and himself had a lovely life. They had two children and he died a happy man.'

But Anne's mother was only fifty-three when she died from breast cancer. 'I didn't know what was wrong, first she fell and fractured her hip, and she was brought into the Adelaide Hospital, the Protestant hospital, and Dr Somerville-Large was the main surgeon there and he did the hip, but she was in bed for years after that and then my father bought a wheelchair and we used to wheel her around.

'We'd go over to the nuns, and you'd go in there and get a glass of milk. It was the Carmelites or the Poor Clares, I don't know which of them. May Tobin and I used to go in and get a glass of milk, just for the cod of it. We didn't need it but we would get the glass of milk and then wheel the poor woman around.'

Anne was twelve when her mother died. 'I don't know how I felt. I was sad but I couldn't express it in any way. Unie cried. I remember sitting on one of the beds and I sat beside him but I didn't cry. She died in Dublin, in James's Hospital, that used to be an awful place at one time but it had improved by then. She was only in for one night and then she died the next day. My father must have gone to the hospital.

'I remember the funeral all right. I was dressed in black and they put a black mantilla on my head. And I remember meeting two girls who said they were sorry about my mother and I said, "It's all right." I didn't know what to say.'

A Fianna Fáil Family

Although the Black and Tans were well gone when Anne was a child, the memory was still strong among her parents' generation. 'My father used to say that he was coming up Rosy Hill – I always remember this story – he was coming up Rosy Hill and he heard the Black and Tans lorry coming. And I remember him saying the hairs stood on the back of his neck with the fright and wondering were they going to shoot him.' But Anne says when she was growing up there was nothing to be frightened of. 'Because we had the Fianna Fáil government, there was Dev and the big marches and the bands. We had a brass and reed band and Colonel Delaney was the conductor. My brother

Jimmy joined the band with the big euphonium, the big 'boom', and then Bob joined it later and played the coronet, the smaller coronet. But Jimmy had no tone, although he could read all the music. They used to play at everything and they'd lead the marches with Fianna Fáil up through Dundrum and everyone would follow them.'

Anne grew up in a Fianna Fáil family. 'My father was a member. He got involved with the Brennans of Dundrum. They lived opposite the old graveyard, they were very good friends of my father.' Anne remembers the election campaigns, 'And going up and listening to them all speaking, not that we were interested as children. But there was always political discussion around the house, my mother and father, and my mother's brothers – Jim, who lived across the road from us, and Paddy from Dundrum itself – they used to come down and they would have big discussions about politics. But they had no time for Cosgrave.'

Even today Anne has a photo of Éamon de Valera on her sitting-room wall. 'I got that from my brother Jack, under great stress I can tell you – he kept saying, "No, you're not getting that," and I'd say, "Ah, Jack, go on." So eventually he relented and got it framed and gave it to me. Nice, isn't it?'

Even today Anne has a photo of
Éamon de Valera on her
sitting-room wall.

Anne has very clear memories of her friends when she was a young woman. 'There were three girls next door, Emily, Sissy and Maeve Lenihan. Maeve was two years older than me and I remember they dressed to kill, and they were dancers, ballroom dancers. Emily got cancer and sadly died very young. She met this fella, we used to call him "the Squire Maguire" from Dún Laoghaire, he used to come out to visit her. Then she went to Lourdes and she came home and died the next day. It was very sad.'

Wheezy Anna

Then there was the 'fancy dancing' taught by a girl from Ranelagh which was followed by Irish dancing taught by Paddy Medlar. Another big attraction was the circus, which visited Dundrum every second year, 'with the hurdy gurdies in the intervening years'.

'The circus was held in the field next to Dundrum

Asylum. It was magical. There was a circus girl, Babette. Now I know I was young and innocent but we were told that she had had all the bones taken out of her body. That's how she was able to bend back and do all these acrobatics.

> We were told that she had had all the bones taken out of her body. That's how she was able to bend back and do all these acrobatics.

'Then they held a contest one year, for everybody who could sing or dance or anything. My friend May Tobin and myself, we got up and did a reel. We were about nine at the time. But the winner was a girl we called Wheezy Anna, after the song she sang. The prize was based on the applause you got and of course the lads clapped and clapped and she won the prize. Later she joined the pipe band from Churchtown, but after that night she never went by anything other than Wheezy Anna.

'She was one of the Phelans who were in the printing business in Windy Arbour. She met her husband in the band and, after the wedding, the whole band walked down the street and they were dressed in their uniform. I was delighted with all this carry-on. They had a bit of a hooley later on, and the music went on all night. But there's a sequel to this – that song never left me. I always thought of Wheezy Anna. She married that chap and I lost touch when I married at twenty-one.'

In later years, Anne became an accomplished dancer, so much so that she appeared on a Pathé newsreel.

Anne says she discovered boys when she was about ten. 'We all played on the road and one of the games involved having to kiss a boy and the young fella that I kissed had a snotty nose and I never played that game again. I hated it. And to make it worse, he was Wheezy Anna's brother's son.'

At the time, most children left school at around twelve years of age. 'All the girls at that time went to Dundrum or Milltown laundry to work, and that's the truth. But my brother Jack said, "Anne's not going to any laundry."

'My father then decided to go away to England to find work. At this stage, all the other boys were married; my mother lived to see them all paired off. But my father had gone away so the question was, where was I going to continue school? Somebody suggested the Rathmines College of Commerce, so my father sent the fees over from England and my bus money and I went there for four or five years. My eldest brother's wife, Kitty, looked after me, she was very good.'

Anne's dad never came home, except for a holiday. 'And I want to tell you a funny one. My brother Jack said, "When I saw him with the brown hat, I knew he meant business." And Jack was right. My father had married his landlady. He just got married, never told us, the reason was that she was very good to him. Very kind to him. And he brought her over here. I was married at this stage. The years go by, they slip by. And he was happy.

'We were only barely moved into this house in 1948, we had very little in the house when we came. My father was very upset. He said, "The little girl is out there in that place and she has nothing." He was worried about me, but sure I was happy as Larry, I had my husband, Frank.'

Roses from a Bus

This brings us to the great romance of Anne's life. When she was eighteen, she got a job in a men's outfitters in Camden Street and started serving her

Anne and Frank, 1945.

apprenticeship. 'I started working for five shillings a week. My father sent my bus fare over and then the brothers pooled together and bought me a bike and I used to cycle into work. I loved the job. I loved it.'

But then Frank Kennedy came on the scene. He was a bus driver, and as Anne cycled to and from work, 'Frank would throw a rose at me from the cab window and I would get off the bike and pick it up. That's how it all started.' Frank arranged his first date with Anne for the following Monday evening, to meet at the Ballast Office.

But then Frank Kennedy came on
the scene. He was a bus driver, and
as Anne cycled to and from work,
'Frank would throw a rose at me from
the cab window and I would get
off the bike and pick it up. That's
how it all started.

Anne's best friends at the time were Maureen
Keogh who worked in Clerys and Ollie Owens
who worked in Nicholls, all of them serving
their apprenticeships. Anne was about twenty
at the time, and was 'a bag of nerves about this
date with this man'. So all three of them went on
the date together. They spotted him on D'Olier
Street. 'I couldn't look over. "He has a brown hat
on," they said. I said, "Keep walking, girls, keep
walking." And they said, "No, go on, he's standing
over there." So he made a dash over and he said
hello to the girls and we went to the cinema, the
Corinthian, I think. We went in and he held my
hand, that's all.

'I had arranged with the girls that we would
get the bus home together. So when we came out

of the cinema we walked up Grafton Street to the Green – that's where I said I would meet the girls at ten – and they were there. Frank kissed me on the forehead and headed off, and me and the girls laughed the whole way home.'

The couple were married two years later with the reception in a hotel in Harcourt Street. Anne's father didn't come home for the wedding.

Frank was a widower and he had two little girls, aged ten and twelve. They lived with their grandmother, his wife's mother, Granny Fennell. His wife died when she was only twenty-four. 'When Jack found out I was going out with Frank, somebody told him that I was going out with a married man. I remember being very upset when he confronted me, I was crying and saying, "He's not married, his wife is dead." Jack was doing the father and mother and he was my minder!

'Granny Fennell was a big part of my life in the beginning. When Frank's wife died, she already had two little girls, Maisie and Lily, belonging to another daughter who had died when giving birth to them. She had those two little girls and then she took in Maureen and Dolores, Frank's two. And she reared them and there was no way she was letting them go. She made me so welcome. She was so good to me, so nice. She was an old woman. Her husband was dead by the time I married Frank. We all got on so well.'

Anne and Frank had four boys: Tony, Noel, Fran and Viv. 'All boys. And Granny Fennell ... I have to tell you about this. When Tony was born, she wanted to see the baby. Then when he got to a certain age where he was kind of walking around, she said, "Don't call him Tony. Anthony. Tony is a horse's name." Tony went down to her then and slept in his granny's bed and slept there every weekend. She loved him.'

Margaret Fennell died when she was in her eighties. Of the four granddaughters she reared, Dolores is still alive, a resident in a nursing home in Galway. Her sister Maureen was killed in a car accident. 'That was the biggest tragedy. Maureen was so lovely. She was married and had three kids. They're married themselves now, Derek, Elaine and Michelle.' Anne became very close with them, 'Oh for God's sake, didn't I take over, they're mad about me, they call me Nana.

'Dolores married a fella called Jackie Leonard and they moved to Galway and lived in Threadneedle Road and, for the past couple of years, Jackie has been in the nursing home with Dolores. Dolores loves living in the nursing home and being waited on. She's in a room of her own and she says, "Anne, its lovely."'

Much of Anne's youth was overshadowed by the Second World War. 'Unie joined up and Bob joined up, he left his job and joined up. Bob didn't join the army part, he was in the kitchen and he used to come home with a few tea bags in his pocket, they were on ration, you know.

'I remember the air-raid shelters around O'Connell Street. I climbed up on one with my pal Madge Cox and she pulled me up to have a look. But I don't think they were ever used.'

Rationing

But it was after the war, she says, when rationing really kicked in.

It was Frank who came to the rescue. 'He had a great way with the Monument Creamery. We used to get the butter there, an ounce of butter. One day, I remember I was low on butter, and I put a little mark onto the card to buy the butter.

I saw the shop girl holding it up and saying, "Mrs Kennedy, I can't give you this butter because it's not right." I was so embarrassed and Frank came in and saw I was so upset. He was a charmer, he went down to the girl and said, "Oh, she got a fright." And she gave him the two ounces of butter.

'And then Granny Fennell used to send me up a half pound of butter every week!'

Holidays were almost unheard of when Anne was young but she recalls one trip to County Wicklow with her next-door neighbours. 'We stayed in tents and I cried all night because I wanted to go home, I didn't like it there in the dark. That's the only holiday I went on.'

Terrified of Confession

Confession is something that Anne remembers well, even her First Confession when she was seven. 'I do remember being terrified and I was bold.' But confession as a young woman was more difficult. 'When I was about eighteen, we used to go to dances up in Ticknock. Maeve Lenihan who lived next door was into dancing and we had to get there either on a bike or by bus. It was a long aul walk. I went there a couple of times. There was a fella called Tommy Feehan in the band and he asked if he could leave me home. And I remember well, on the crossbar of the bike, he said, "Can I kiss you?" I said, "I don't mind." So he kissed me.

'And I remember going to confession in Dundrum church afterwards and saying, "Father, I kissed a boy." And he said, "Was it prolonged?" And I said, "Well ... kind of." I didn't know if it was prolonged or not and he said, "You're making a prostitute of yourself. Stop ... kissing ... around! And be a good girl!" I got a penance, and I did it, but I've no faith in confession. My friend up the road, she goes every week to confession. She doesn't have sins, she's very holy.

'I haven't been to mass in a long time because I'm not very good on the feet. But I know the priest, a lovely priest. I'm not over-religious but I do pray to God every night. I pray, I say the 'Sacred Heart of Jesus' several times a day. I don't sin, I don't lead a bad life, I've no regrets like that.'

Losing Frank, and Finally Grieving

But Anne had a tough time after her beloved Frank died. 'I went to a great doctor down in Seapoint, he'd cure your knee, do acupuncture and I will never forget this as long as I live. This was after Frank died. I went down to this doctor and he sat me down and talked to me and said, "Have you any worries or anything? Any trauma?" I said, "My husband died last year." And he asked me, "Do

Anne and Frank, 1969.

you talk to him?" And I said, "No, not really. Well, we didn't always see eye to eye." And he said, "How long were you married?" And when I told him forty-seven years he said, "Of course you didn't always see eye to eye."

But anyway, he put the needles in my knee and he said he'd leave me there for a while. And I started to cry. I will never forget it to my dying day, how upset I got. And when he came back I was in this awful state. And he said, "Don't worry, that's good for you. Did you cry when Frank died?" And I said, "Well, not really. See, I don't cry easy, I'm not an easy crier." And he said, "I want you to have a little conversation with Frank", and then he walked out.

'And I don't know what came over me but it was awful. And I had to come out and get on a train to come home. And I was in this state on the train and I remember coming into the kitchen and I was like a dog howling. That's the truth. Howling like a dog. But I had not cried. I hadn't grieved for Frank until then.

'When I went back the next day the doctor said, "Well, how are you?" And I said, "Well, I was nearly able to skip down the road. And that is the gospel. It was all the tension, I let everything out. That's the only thing I can think about.'

Anne doesn't like talking about death and the afterlife but we get stuck in anyway. She doesn't like the idea of leaving her family someday and tells me the story of how her brother Jack once gave her a gift of a grave. 'But I said, "Jack, I am going to be buried with Frank." And he says, "Ah, yeah, one under him and one over him," referring to Frank's first wife.'

Jack threatened to talk to her sons about it but he never did.

Admiration for Today's Women

Today Anne is in awe of the wonderful women in her life. She chats about her granddaughters and singles them out as 'very wise' or 'very kind' or 'very independent'. 'They have an independence that my era didn't have. They have a mindset now, they know what they want and it's a good thing. I admire them for it.' Some of her extended family are divorced now and she talks about the good job that the parents have done in rearing their kids between them.

She has a particular soft spot for her grandson, Adrian Kennedy, who is a radio presenter with 98FM. 'I love listening to him.'

1922: Major Events

World

- In Egypt, the tomb of Tutankhamun is discovered in the Valley of the Kings

- The first issue of *Reader's Digest* magazine is published in the USA

- The BBC (British Broadcasting Corporation) is established

- The first successful use of insulin to treat diabetes is carried out in Canada

- Mussolini comes to power in Italy with his National Fascist Party

- Judy Garland and Kingsley Amis are born

Ireland

- The first edition of the newspaper *Poblacht na hÉireann* is published, established by republican opponents to the Anglo-Irish Treaty

- The terms of the Anglo-Irish Treaty are revealed and Éamon de Valera offers his resignation as president of the Republic

- Arthur Griffith is elected President of the Provisional Government and Michael Collins becomes Minister for Finance; de Valera and fifty-six of his supporters walk out of Dáil Éireann

- The government of the United Kingdom releases the remaining Irish prisoners captured during the War of Independence

- Dublin Castle is handed over to the new Provisional Government by the last Viceroy of Ireland

- The Irish Free State (Agreement) Act 1922 is introduced in the British House of Commons

- Existing British postage stamps are issued overprinted with 'Rialtas Sealadach na hÉireann'

- The Civic Guard – predecessor of An Garda Síochána – is established as a police force to replace the Royal Irish Constabulary in areas outside Dublin and Ulster

- The Irish Catholic Church hierarchy implores the people of Ireland to accept the treaty and to make the best of the freedom which it brings

- The final group of British troops leaves the Curragh Camp

- Death of Arthur Griffith, who founded Sinn Féin and led the treaty negotiations in 1921

- Michael Collins is killed in an ambush at Béal na Bláth, County Cork

- The first meeting of the Provisional Parliament takes place at Leinster House; W.T. Cosgrave is elected President of Dáil

Éireann and Chairman of the Provisional Government

- Erskine Childers is executed by firing squad at Beggars Bush Barracks after conviction by an Irish military court for the unlawful possession of a gun

- The Parliament of Northern Ireland votes to remain part of the United Kingdom

- The names of King's County and Queen's County are informally changed to Offaly and Laois respectively

- All-Ireland champions: Kilkenny (hurling) and Dublin (football)

To School on the Pony and Trap

Tom Stack
Born 20 January 1922
Sr Dympna Stack (Eileen)
Born 13 August 1928

Tom and Eileen are the two surviving siblings of the six children born to James and Molly Stack (née Cunningham) in north Kerry in a place called Moyvane, near Listowel. Tom was the eldest, followed by John, May, Eileen, Dick and Bridie. Tom has strong memories of growing up on the family farm. 'There was no electricity until 1932 and no tractors, we ploughed with a horse. It was a mixed farm, dairy and beef, pigs and hens. We killed our own pigs. It was a very enjoyable occasion. We looked forward to it once a year.'

The Meitheal and the Killing of the Pig

'We had what is called a *meitheal* in Irish where the neighbours all clubbed in and helped one another out. As children we thought it very exciting. It

Bringing out churns of milk to Moyvane creamery, 1960s.

was all done manually. My father used to kill a pig roughly once a year, with a knife, a butcher's knife. In some places, the pig was struck with a timber mallet on the forehead but in our place we just used a knife. We very much looked forward to the making of the homemade puddings and pork steak. Those homemade puddings were the nicest you've ever had in your life. And, of course, we didn't have meat most of the year, so it was especially welcome on that account.

'Everyone helped out. There was no running water, so the children used to go down to the well which was half a mile away and bring back buckets of water, which were boiled on an open kitchen fire in a big pot. It had to be boiling hot for the shaving and the cleaning of the pig. We shared the food of the freshly killed pig with the neighbours, everybody who helped. One pig would last the year.' The family also grew their own vegetables and Tom's mother made the bread – griddled bread and soda cake. 'They were good days. It was hard work but we didn't feel it. We enjoyed each other's company. We were easily pleased. It was easy to feed us, we liked the simple things in life. We had a lovely kitchen, an open fire with a wide chimney in

Dick Stack, Tom's brother, in front of the thatched homestead at Moyvane, 1968, pictured with his wife Sheila, three of Tom's children and their cousin Ann McCarthy on the trap. Deirdre Stack is holding the reins.

the actual room. A very big kitchen and a very busy kitchen.'

The primitive conditions – by today's standards – didn't bother the children. 'In the summer we would bathe in the river that ran through the land. And for the ordinary day-to-day washing, we had to rely on the open fire in the kitchen. There was a lot of poverty, there were no rich people, but there was a great spirit of generosity.'

'People were very religious back then, I heard an expression used quite recently, in jest of course: "We robbed and we plundered, but we never lost the faith." We were all afraid of the priest. It was frightening, although we didn't realise it at the time. There was a local teacher, a local garda and the local priest, and we were afraid of our life of all of them. If we saw or heard about them walking the roads, we would hide until they passed by.'

There was a local teacher, a local
garda and the local priest, and we
were afraid of our life of all of them.
If we saw or heard about
them walking the roads, we would
hide until they passed by.

Father on the Run

Tom was always conscious of his father's republican background. 'They were terrible times. My father was an IRA man as much as anybody else was. A lot of it was secret but he never went to prison. His wedding day was a non-event. They got married all right, they went to the church in a

James and Molly Stack in Moyvane, 1964.

pony and trap. It was a lovely mass, I believe, with cousins and relations and they had a lovely time. There were no hotels, the wedding breakfast was in the home, there were special things to eat and a bit of dancing on the kitchen floor. But the groom had to slip away as the Black and Tans were after him. Most men were classified as rebels so he went on the run.

He escaped onto the land and hid himself; it was a fair-sized farm so he went as far as he could from the public road to make it hard to find him. They didn't catch him. He would have been a marked man, same as any man, because of his age. But he came home and went back to farming and he continued his IRA activities.

> There were no hotels, the wedding
> breakfast was in the home, there
> were special things to eat and a bit of
> dancing on the kitchen floor. But the
> groom had to slip away as the Black
> and Tans were after him.

'He hardly ever talked about his involvement in the IRA. I suppose in that environment, it's only natural to keep your mouth to yourself and not be spreading news that might be used as evidence against you. You see you had the IRA, which was the origin of the independent state and naturally they were rebellious from time to time, especially during the era of the Black and Tans. There were a lot of things happening locally – shootings, assassinations. There would be congregations on the anniversaries of someone's death, and that was the impact of the War of Independence on

the locality. Each locality had their own reasons for remembering 1916, not because they had any real knowledge of Michael Collins or anyone like him, but because there would be some other local person who took the same risk and fought the same war as Michael Collins, if that makes sense.

'It was only a few years after the founding of Dáil Éireann in 1919. So they were exciting times. When the election was over, there were plenty of bonfires. As kids, we took pleasure in those too. And talking about bonfires, a great attraction in most of the country was greyhound racing. We had a local greyhound dog that won the Irish Cup in Clonana and there was great excitement. The name of the dog was Dainty Man, and there was great enjoyment about the winning of his trophy.'

They travelled everywhere by pony and cart. Primary school was about a mile away, across back roads. 'We went by bike. Secondary school – St Michael's in Listowel – was six miles away and we cycled that too. I did my Leaving Cert and then I got a scholarship and went to University College Cork and studied civil engineering. I did a Bachelor of Arts before that because I was thinking of teaching but some of my friends who were already

Tom's graduation from
University College Cork.

teaching advised me not to, so I changed to engineering. So now I have two degrees.'

But jobs were scarce and Tom worked with various county councils before joining the then Department of Industry and Commerce. One of his major projects there was the construction of the main runway at Dublin airport.

Valentine's Day Wedding

Tom came to live and work in Ennis, County Clare, in 1952. At that time a young woman, Joan Murphy, was the manager of Carmody's, a local hotel. 'It was a famous hotel where, on one occasion, the first floor collapsed with the weight of the people in one room. There was a fire lit in the room and the fireplace came down and all, with the fire lit in it. It was during an auction but before my time. Eight people were killed.'

Tom had already met Joan several years earlier

at an event in Cork City. 'She was one of the staff down there and she reminded me of that in later years.' But there was no spark on that occasion. 'We clicked when she worked in Carmody's Hotel. I was enjoying myself in Ennis, working as a civil engineer. I was in Carmody's quite often and I got talking to her and I asked her out on a date. We went to the pictures.'

The couple were married on Valentine's Day, 1957. Tom is eleven years older than Joan. I ask him if he remembers buying the engagement ring. 'It was a non-event. I didn't get one bit excited about it.'

'I'm surprised this woman married you.'

'I'm surprised myself at times!'

The couple have five children: Deirdre, Eileen, James, Pauline and Tom Junior.

Joan came from Cork, near Kanturk, and had two sisters, Kitty and Teresa. As young girls, they travelled to primary school on a pony and trap, with Joan in charge of the horse. Kitty became a secondary-school teacher in Sligo and Teresa joined the Ursulines and became a nun. 'She hated the habit because she was very attractive and very good-looking and you could never imagine her with this menagerie on her head and face,' their daughter Deirdre tells me. 'And then she went to Georgia for a number of years, and sadly she got diagnosed with cancer and came home to die. Kitty passed away as well.'

Teresa was living on the family farm in Cork. 'So my mum lost two sisters and both her parents all in the space of something like three and a half years in the early eighties, it was a tsunami of grief for her.' Joan left Ennis then, to temporarily go down to the home place in Cork because everything was left up in the air. Kitty had been managing the farm and looking after the farm. She had never married. So my mum went down and literally just put on another hat and went farming. She even started sheep farming, there were never sheep down there. It was amazing. Dad used to drive down to Cork as much as he could. And it just seemed so romantic.'

Sadly, Joan has had health problems in recent years and is now being cared for.

Thoughts on Modern Ireland

Tom's career flourished and he spent most of his working life, from 1952 until 1986, as Chief Fire Officer for County Clare. So what does he think of Ireland today? 'The people are way, way better off. We had absolutely no money, hence birthdays didn't mean anything to us. There was nobody that you could mark out as rich or poor, everybody had much the same standard. Anybody who had a bit more than others, they shared what they had, and that's how people got through their farming or whatever work they were in, they depended on the co-operation of neighbours. But, on the whole, I would say Ireland is better today. People are more independent now than they were then.'

Tom's sister Eileen, however, says she is sad about the modern Ireland. 'We are becoming totally non-Christian from the top down. We are losing where we came from. We have lost a lot of values. I would be open about a lot of things, and the birth of children is so precious. I don't mind what the circumstances of the conception, but to think about aborting a child …. And now they are talking about what went on in Tuam, and I would love to ask the Minister for Children – they're rooting up all these children and spending money on giving them graves – what about the aborted children? What are they doing about those babies? They are as precious as the ones that are born. Only God can create a life.'

And now they are talking about what
went on in Tuam, and I would love
to ask the Minister for Children –
they're rooting up all these children
and spending money on giving them
graves – what about the aborted
children? What are they doing about
those babies? They are as precious
as the ones that are born. Only God
can create a life.

'All Virgin Births!'

Eileen has strong views about Tuam and what
happened there. 'I think they are forgetting the
history there. All virgin births! No word about a
dad or the families. There are young people who
didn't live through that, and they think it's the same
as today. But where would those girls have gone?
I remember when I was a child, a neighbouring
woman, whose daughter was pregnant out of
marriage, came to the house one day and she
was crying in the kitchen. I remember being put

outside the door and listening at the door, and this woman was in an awful state. And I remember my father saying to that woman, "Mary, you will have that child look after your family yet." Wasn't he ahead of his time? I never forgot that. I was still in national school when that happened, but I was curious as to what this hidden thing going on in the kitchen was.'

Eileen recalls a stillborn birth in her own family in the mid-thirties, her mother's seventh child. 'I remember the doctor coming in the middle of the night and my father racing and running around. And there was a dead-born baby. A box was made, and that baby was buried on the verge of the grave, the Stack graves, the very next day. There were many children then that died soon after birth.'

Eileen is now Sr Dympna of the Sisters of the Christian Retreat, a congregation 'founded at the time of the French Revolution, 1789', Eileen tells me. 'By a rural parish priest who believed that the world was becoming a desert for want of reflection. He founded it to help people meditate. I was the first to come here, to Mountbellew, in 1965.'

School Memories – and Early Thoughts of Religious Life

Eileen's earliest memory is when she was in Fifth Class and was asked to take a child from a local family to school with her. 'I would pick her up in the morning at the gate and I thought it was so lovely to be going to school with this little child, just holding her hand and walking to school. It was about a mile to school. School was okay – we had a boys' school and a girls' school on the same grounds but they never mixed across the yard. The principal could be tough, she was a bit hard on us at times. The boys' school was better. Tom was good at Irish. The principal of the boys' school was the husband of the principal of the girls' school, and he was a great Irish speaker. They spoke Irish fluently, but the girls' school didn't have much Irish.'

After primary school, Eileen went to Moyderwell in Tralee, run by the Mercy Sisters. 'It was what they called a secondary top – a glorified national school that went on to Leaving Cert. There were no fees there. My older sister, May, went to the Presentation in Listowel, cycled in the five or six miles. My mother had a lot of relations in the Presentation order, and I was in secondary with the Mercy Sisters because my father had a sister in the Mercy Sisters, and he had a niece who was in that school already. So I was sent to Tralee, which meant I stayed in digs with other youngsters in a house, at age fourteen. We enjoyed it, but the only thing was, Tralee had terrible poverty at that time, and there would be girls in the school out of slums. I remember side roads you would be afraid to go down, you wouldn't dream of walking down them. It was a big change from Moyvane.'

Eileen says she had thought of the religious life when she was very young. 'I remember coming home from devotions on Good Friday, and hearing the Passion story, and I remember asking, "Why didn't Jesus come down from the cross and murder all those people that were nailing him to the cross? Why did he let them do that?" I remember standing in the yard and saying that. A bit of violence in me. But I thought, *Why didn't he do something about it? Why did he let them, and forgive them, and say "Father, they know not what they do?"* I would have been ten or eleven then, around Confirmation age.'

When she did her Leaving Certificate, she wanted to be a teacher. 'As a small child I used to teach the stones outside the back door. That was my hobby. But at that time, to get into primary teaching – there was no question of university, that was too expensive – you had to pass a singing test, a music test. I hadn't a note in my head, and a good nun from Tralee tried to teach me a bit. I did the test and I failed hopelessly. So that was it.

'A friend of mine had gone to England and discovered that if you taught as a student in a school – somebody would take you on, for two years, and your Leaving Cert was good enough – you could then apply to go to college over there.'

Eileen ended up with the Sisters of the Christian Retreat in Surrey. 'It was a boarding school and a day school, and I could stay in the school. I could get something like two pounds a week.' Later, she went to a teacher training college in London.

She was very taken by the sisters and their work in a school that welcomed pupils of every religion, with boarders from Iran and Iraq. 'Remember this was a Catholic school they were running. They were very good to all these people of all backgrounds, poor people as well, even though it was a fee-paying school. I remember a family from Ireland coming over, three girls, they didn't pay any fees but because they were Catholic they were taken in. They were day pupils, they weren't borders. I was amazed at the relationship between the pupils and the sisters. They got on well together. The principal was a wonderful woman, an Englishwoman.

'We had English girls there as well, and some of them are still writing to me. I get cards from twenty or so people from all over the world.'

Going to France Is 'Not On'

'I decided to enter the convent and the novitiate was in France. I had to go home to tell my parents and my father said, "If you went to America or New Zealand, I wouldn't mind because they speak English there, but going to France is not on."' But she joined up anyway, in 1949.

'I had to learn French. I wasn't gifted at languages. There were four of us together from Ireland, and we would use the odd bit of English. It was tough, France was tough, different culture altogether and the language was a big problem. I didn't like getting up early in the morning either, I had to get up at 5 a.m.'

Eileen's first profession was in February 1952. Later, she went back to England dressed in a white habit. 'We had a black habit for going out and for work, and a white habit for prayers and choir for Sunday. It hadn't a veil, it had blinkers, so you couldn't see sideways.' Her father said nothing more about it. 'I suppose he accepted me after that.'

Eileen's first visit home was for ten days in 1964 and her parents met her at Limerick. Her father wasn't well then and died the following year. She was principal of a school in east Surrey at that stage. 'I remember coming home for his funeral and being met at Shannon airport by a neighbour and being very upset. The wake was in the house. I wasn't used to that, we didn't have wakes in England.'

In 1965, Eileen was transferred to Mountbellew where she spent twenty-five years as principal of the Holy Rosary College. Even when she left teaching, you couldn't really say she had retired. Would she consider herself retired even now, I asked her. 'No, I probably wouldn't. I drive down to the shops and get the messages in the morning after we say our prayers. At the moment, I am doing a bit of work on the family history and putting together these photos. I'm not good on the computer but I can do a bit.'

As a nun, I expected Eileen to believe in an afterlife, and she does. 'We will be back home.

Life wouldn't be worth living if there wasn't an afterlife. We would just rot and that's it. I hope I will meet all my relations, my parents, my sisters and a lot of past pupils who have died. I wouldn't be ready for death yet but I am getting there. I know my age. I have to accept it when it comes but I say, "Lord, leave me my head, whatever about my legs." I am not ready to die yet but I may be taken any time.'

Sr Dympna died on 13 March 2020. May she rest in peace.

The Shoe on the Anvil

Bridget Josephine Maguire
Born 15 September 1922

'The big house, the cement-tiled floors, the big black range. That's where I worked. I was eighteen and I came up to work in 1941, just before Christmas. I had to do everything and anything, washing, the sheets and all. They had to be soaked the night before, they wouldn't be as dirty as on a farm, though. The family were farmers too but they were yuppie farmers. There were no modern appliances, just a sweeping brush and a mop. You got down on your knees to do the floor, it's no wonder I have two arthritic knees. The exercise was supposed to be good for them.

'I learned how to cook there. The lady of the house used to cook, but she told me I had to peel the spuds and the cabbage and carrots and all that, I had to do all the hard work and she did the clean work, putting it into the pots. She cooked sirloin roast, bacon, they didn't do their own bacon, they bought it from a butcher that did all that. There was lamb, they must have killed their own lambs and chicken. They ate all that but they gave very little to me. It was very bad, I used to be picking at the roast when I got the chance, to get a little bit into me. They paid me but you wouldn't get enough, I got twenty-five pounds a year.'

Bridie Maguire was born at home. 'In my own house in the small village of Drimeyra, between Killimer, Ballinasloe, Loughrea and Portumna. It was more of a townland really.

'There was nine of us. I was the eldest and the mammy of them all. Brendan was next to me, then Ina, Fred, Kathleen, Gertie, Gerard, Christina and Josephine. There's only four of us left. Two went within three months of each other. The three brothers, they were bachelors. Kathleen, who lives here in Meath, is still alive, she's only eighty-eight, a young one compared to me. Josephine is the youngest, she's only seventy-nine.'

Bridie's parents were Thomas Larkin and Katie Coyne. 'My mother's family were farmers and they had just the two daughters. My mother's sister got married and she got the home place. That time, the man went into the house if the woman had a place. She inherited the farm.'

Her Father the Farrier

Bridie's father was a farrier. 'A blacksmith, shoeing horses for the hunts. I remember all the people coming, he would be down on the farm and one of us that was capable would be sent down to call him up. The forge was big enough and there was the anvil where they hammered out the shoes. They made the shoes with a big sheet of iron. He had a coal fire, special coal. There was no such thing as a coal fire in the house then, it was turf or peat or wood. I can still see him turning the shoe on the anvil, beating it out to size. I remember him going back to fit it to the horse's hoof.'

They made the shoes with a big sheet of iron. He had a coal fire, special coal. There was no such thing as a coal fire in the house then, it was turf or peat or wood. I can still see him turning the shoe on the anvil, beating it out to size. I remember him going back to fit it to the horse's hoof.

Bridie recalls the forge as a good business. 'My mother used to have a little red notebook and she would write down everything. Them times, most of them wouldn't have the money to pay there and then, some of them did. It was half a crown for the four new shoes on the horses. I can remember I used to write it down in later years.

'Then they used to take off the shoes when they got worn down, and recycle them, bring them up better, so they wouldn't slip on the frost on the road.'

The farm itself was 'good land for Galway', she says. 'We had forty-nine acres which was good in those days. We kept cattle and sheep and we had two horses, for ploughing and that. We grew oats, wheat, potatoes, turnips. We had hens, chickens, pigs. The younger ones didn't like the pigs, they were ugly-looking things. We killed a pig on the farm and ate it, it kept us going.'

From School to Earning a Living

When Bridie was six she started at the local school, which was about a mile down the road. 'We had cousins living nearer to the school and the church, and I was brought down there on the Sunday evening, to my aunt's house. Her eldest

Bridget on the morning of her first day at work.

daughter was a year older than me and she brought me to school for the week. I stayed with them for the first week but then I had to paddle my own canoe and walk to school from home. It was a mile, but you could go across fields. That was nicer than going on the road. We wore shoes when we were first starting, but as time went on, we used to wear the little plastic sandals with a T-bar.'

She has very good memories of her schooldays. 'It was a very good school. The teacher was very good, as good as some secondary teachers. I learned algebra and geometry, I was quite good at that, you know.' Bridie then introduced all her brothers and sisters to school. 'I was kind of the mother to them. I did a lot for them and the ones that are left still look up to me as the mother.'

She left school at sixteen and was at home for a while. 'Then this cousin of mine, the one who had brought me to school and that, she had gone to work, she got into a hotel when she was sixteen or seventeen. I wanted to be like the other girls in my class and work. So I went to do housework in one of the big mansions they had years ago.'

This is where she earned £25 a year, but her parents helped to support her too. 'Your parents would give you something when you went home. But you don't realise, them times the money was worth a lot more, half a crown was worth a lot of money. I was seven years with that family and then the son was getting married and he hitched his mother up to Dublin, to an apartment, and I was sent with her. It was in Rathmines. She was very nice to me then; she used to bring me into the city once a week and we would have tea in Mitchells Café or Bewleys Café. She used to shop in Switzers, those big shops.'

But Bridie didn't like the life in Dublin. 'Eventually one of my sisters came up too and I got her a place with a dentist in Ranelagh so I had that bit of company. But, unfortunately, only a year later, I got up one morning and my employer was shouting for her life, for her breath. She'd had a heart attack and died. I really knew nobody. I was nineteen, she was probably only seventy, which is young today.'

Bridie had several other jobs, mostly working as a housekeeper. But one position was with a doctor. 'I was the house maid, the door maid, everything. My wages had gone up probably by a fiver. But there was an awful lot you could do with that ... the grand coats I used to buy. I used to save up. They'd be far better than the coats now, the quality was better, they would last longer. You'd get a coat and it would last two years.'

'I Picked One with a Car and a Bit of Land'

Bridie was working in Trim, County Meath, when she met her husband, Tom Maguire. 'That was the end of my working days. My sister had a boyfriend and it ended up that we all met up and went down the country, there used to be house dances, a party, a dance round the kitchen and there would be someone playing music. Through that, we met our husbands, both of us, they were first cousins.'

And she remembers clearly the day Tom proposed to her. 'My father was alive at the time. Tom came down just before Christmas. He had only been coming down about a year. And he said, "My mother is gone now and I don't want to be on my own." He was hopeless on his own, he hated not being in company.

Bridget and Tom's wedding.

And he said, "I was wondering, would you marry me?" And I said, "I'll have to think about that." So we kind of forgot about it for a while and one day he said, "Would you make up your mind!" So I said, "I think I will, but I might kick you out yet."

'Then Tom said, "I've got to ask your father. Will you tell him, and then I'll ask him, can I." My father was glad I was going to marry someone, I would say. I was working and living in Meath at that stage. So we used to go up and down.' Tom had a car. 'I picked one with a car and a bit of land, as they say. We only had a small wedding. My mother was dead. Anyway, we had about forty at the wedding. We got married on the thirtieth of December, why then I don't know. He didn't want to wait any longer. A winter wedding. I wore a suit, a costume they called it. It was lovely, I wish I had kept it. It was creamy, like a tweed, with a yellowy flick in it. And I had a blue hat. The reception was in Hayden's Hotel in Ballinasloe, a beautiful hotel. We got married at ten o'clock in the morning, and they used to call it a breakfast afterwards but it was a full dinner, most beautifully presented. They don't present them like that now, I wish someone had videoed it.'

The couple went to Belfast for their honeymoon. 'You'll begin to think, *This is the queerest one I've ever met*. Belfast! And it was 1964, so just before the Troubles, but it was bad at that time too. My husband had a cousin up there, so that's where we went. We spent a week. We stayed with the cousins, they had a very big house near the Falls Road. We never saw any trouble but when I thought of it afterwards ...

Adjusting to a Life Without Children

'I married into a farm, about thirty-five acres. I was thirty-nine when I got married. It's like that now, girls marrying later but, in them times, it was terrible to get married at that age because you might not have children.'

Bridie did become pregnant but lost her baby in the early stages of the pregnancy. 'I was in Holles Street for three or four weeks. It was traumatic. I often think what might have been, but my husband used to say, to console ourselves, "Ah, sure, what about it, maybe he or she would be a divil and throw us out or something!" It's only as we got older that we thought of that. I always thought it was a boy, myself. I don't know why. You wouldn't know at that stage.'

The doctors told Bridie she couldn't have another baby. 'So I just adjusted to it because there was a lot of that at the time.' She tried to adopt, but it didn't work out. 'I was too old to adopt. You had to be no older than thirty, I think. I was forty-one or so.' She says she feels she missed out by not having children, but is philosophical. 'As you get older … it's past tense.'

> She feels she missed out by not
> having children, but is philosophical.
> 'As you get older … it's past tense.'

Losing Tom

Bridie and Tom had a good life together. 'We used to go up and down to my home place in Galway. I had two bachelor brothers and Tom loved going down to them and the farm and doing bits for them. I used to bring the cattle in for them.' Tom died at the age of eighty-seven from lung cancer. 'He was a smoker and he was a dirty smoker, as I used to say. You know when he'd be working with the tractor and he would light a cigarette and he'd be puffing away.'

After Tom died, Bridie says she just lived on the best she could. 'I rented the land, it is still rented. I still have my house. I'm only six months in the nursing home here [Woodlands Nursing Home in Navan]. I thought when I came in, I would be able to go home. But not now, because it is so hard with doctors and getting home help and all. I haven't gone to visit my house yet but maybe next week, now that the weather is better.'

Asked about how she views Ireland today, Bridie says, 'I think it's bad, I'll tell you, compared to my time. We had more friends, more time for chatting, talking ... do you think someone would chat for the length of time you're talking? Them times they'd sit for hours, talking to you, they would say, "I'm only staying a minute" and they'd stay for two hours chatting to you. I can't understand it now.'

Few Regrets

Bridie has few regrets but says she probably would have liked to go and see her sisters in England more than she did. 'I didn't travel much, only to England and to Lourdes once. My husband wouldn't go on a plane. He was a big brave man, he was six feet tall and I was only a little thing, but he was frightened of planes and boats. He didn't go to Lourdes with me, I went on a pilgrimage.'

And the advice she has for young people? 'Try and keep in touch with your parents and look after them and spend the most time you can with them because you won't always have them. I was only twenty-nine when my mother died and, at that time, I thought she was an old woman, but she was only fifty-three.'

In terms of religion, Bridie says, 'I'm not a Holy Mary but I am religious in my own way. I pray.' So, what about an afterlife? 'With the way people talk in this present day, they're beginning to put me off that there's an afterlife. But I hope there is. To think I've spent all this life being good and there's nothing at the end. I do believe in God but, as Gay Byrne says, who is He?'

Bridie isn't overly concerned by death. 'I talk about it. I know I have to die. I used to think when I was younger, that when I become such an age I will think, *I'm old, when will I die? Will I die tomorrow?* and all that, but I can't imagine now when or how or where I am going to die. It doesn't frighten me now. I know I am near. I can't go on forever.'

1923: Major Events

World

- Mount Etna on Sicily erupts and 60,000 people are made homeless

- The world's first domestic refrigerator is sold in Sweden

- Warner Brothers establishes a film studio on Sunset Boulevard in Hollywood

- First issue of *Time* magazine is published in the USA

- The first Le Mans twenty-four-hour race is held in France

- Charlton Heston is born

Ireland

- Beechpark, the residence of President W.T. Cosgrave in Dublin, is set on fire

- Minister for Education Eoin MacNeill announces that Irish is to become a subject for examination in the civil service

- The government releases two captured documents issued by the IRA – the letters, signed by Éamon de Valera and Frank Aiken (the new Chief of Staff), call for the dumping of arms and the ending of armed struggle; the Civil War is officially over

- In the general election, Cumann na nGaedheal under W.T. Cosgrave win most seats and form a minority government

- Ireland is admitted to the League of Nations

- The Fourth Dáil meets for the first time at Leinster House; Michael Hayes is elected Ceann Comhairle and W.T. Cosgrave is elected President of the Executive Council

- The Nobel Prize for Literature is awarded to poet and playwright W.B. Yeats

- All-Ireland champions: Galway (hurling) and Dublin (football)

A Huguenot Legacy

Charlie Fitzmahony
Born 17 November 1923

I was born in the year 1632, in the
city of York, of a good family, though
not of that country ...

The opening lines of Daniel Defoe's *Robinson Crusoe* and one of the earliest memories of Charlie Fitzmahony. 'I was the baby of the family and I remember my mother tucking me in and reading a bit of *Robinson Crusoe* every night.'

He has other bedtime memories as well, including climbing out of his cot when he was just two and a half and making it all the way into his parents' bed. 'I made a few attempts to get out but I can remember exactly the day I succeeded, getting my foot up and dragging myself up and out. Mother and Father were in the bed and I can remember crawling up and getting in between them.'

Charlie's mother was May Power and his father was Maurice 'Mossie' Fitzmahony. The couple had ten children: Jenny, Frankie, Gerald, Louis, twins Raymond and Geraldine, Marie, Betty, Pauline, and the baby, Charlie. His mother was a great pianist and had a piano. She had lived in France for a time and taught English and she kept in contact down through the years as letters postmarked with a French stamp arrived regularly from a friend there.

A Huguenot Legacy

These early memories come from the post office on the Main Street in Portarlington where Charlie's father was the postmaster. He describes the old Huguenot building where he can recall every room and every twist and turn of the tall French-built house. 'It was a bit unusual but it's still there today. The windows might be a bit different, it has been brought up to date, but it is a most unusual house.'

Indeed Portarlington itself has a most unusual history, a town where the Huguenots arrived with their own stonemasons and gardeners to renovate the homes that lay derelict after the various feuds.

And where just one hundred years earlier, you could hear French spoken on the streets.

Charlie has a photographic memory of the children he played with on Foxcroft Lane, where the street was their playground. 'Across the road from us there were the Sheedys, two boys, Jack and Phil, then there was Arthur, whose dad drove an oil lorry. We didn't mix that much with the Huguenot or Protestant families. Lecumbers lived around the corner, Lofty and Violet were the girls' names. One of their favourite games was called 'cuck', a version of hide and seek.

> Indeed Portarlington itself has a
> most unusual history, a town where
> the Huguenots arrived with their
> own stonemasons and gardeners to
> renovate the homes that lay derelict
> after the various feuds. And
> where just one hundred years earlier
> you could hear French spoken
> on the streets.

Charlie didn't play football but he wanted to be a hurler. 'I remember one time we had the sports in the school and I was tipped to win; I was very good at running but Johnny Mooney was a better runner than me on the day, and he got the first prize which was a medal. As the runner-up, I got a hurley and a ball. I was delighted with myself when I won that. I didn't want the medal but he wanted my hurley and ball so he offered to make an exchange. I said no.'

Politics, TB, Poverty and School

When Charlie was eight there was a general election, on 16 February 1932. It was the first election to be held since the British government had granted full independence to the Irish Free State. 'I remember Dev coming and speaking in the Square, there was a big rally and people gathered around but I couldn't tell you what he was talking about.'

Tuberculosis, also known as TB or consumption, was the scourge of the country from the 1920s onwards. 'It was terrible, if it got into a household it went through the family. My own brother Gerry died from it in the fifties. He had got it years earlier and spent a lot of time in a sanatorium in Newcastle in County Wicklow. There was a veranda with a row of beds and they all had TB. They were put out on the veranda to get the fresh air.'

Charlie also remembers the poverty around Portarlington when he was a boy. 'There was a woman who died of starvation. She was very gaunt and used to come to our house. She lived in a hut out on the bog.'

There was a woman who died of starvation. She was very gaunt and used to come to our house. She lived in a hut out on the bog.

He does not have very good memories of his schooldays. 'The first teacher I had wasn't too bad but I hated going to school. I remember my first day there. I was six years old and the teacher, John Kenny, came to me and said, "Who would you like to sit beside?" I was late going to school that morning and sure I didn't know most of them. I did know Tom and Jack Flaherty, the sons of the local sergeant, they lived in the barracks only across the road from us. So I said I'd like to sit beside Jack.

Charlie (in his father's arms) with his parents and eight of
his nine siblings.

'There was a blackboard and the teacher had
this big yoke with big pages and he'd hang it on
the blackboard to teach us Irish. There was a ring
– a *fáinne* – and cheese – *cáis* – and he would turn
over these pages till we learned the words. We had
a special headline copy for writing, maybe they
still have them. We lived very near the school so,
at lunchtime, someone would collect me on a bike
and bring me home for çocoa and bread.'

Charlie remembers the cruel punishments doled out by some teachers. 'One of them lashed us with a leather strap. Years later, when I was working as an electrician, I had this young fella working with me and he says he had this terrible teacher, and wasn't it the same teacher. He used to lash the hell out of us.

'And even when we weren't in school, we were being watched. You wouldn't miss mass but every month on a Sunday, we had to go to devotions at three o'clock. It was a killer. But sometimes we'd be out hunting rabbits and we missed it, and then got slapped for missing it. We were brought to confession regularly from an early age. I remember my childhood sins well because I made them up. We all made them up.'

But even parents were quick to chastise their children. Charlie remembers one incident at home when he decided to throw a potato from the dinner table onto the floor, announcing that he didn't want those aul potatoes any more. 'I threw it down and my father got the stick and started to chase me. I remember my two sisters, they opened the door into the scullery and rescued me.'

Parcels from America
and Black Turkeys

First Communion was very important and Charlie remembers getting a suit from an aunt in America for the occasion. 'God bless America for the clothes parcels,' he says. 'I made my First Communion in a suit that came from America. It had a lovely jacket with frills at the back of it. And knickerbockers. All the fashion in America at the time, although my mother got a local seamstress to take the frills off the jacket before I wore it.'

There were a number of aunts in America and one in South Africa who also sent parcels home. She was Aunt Meg, a nurse in the First World War. She had been in the trenches and her hearing was badly damaged and she was in bad health when the war was over. She went to live in South Africa thinking the climate would be better. She became a matron in a hospital in Johannesburg.'

At Christmas, the Fitzmahonys always got a turkey from the Jesuit Novitiate in Emo. 'Because my father had a lot of coming and going from the novitiate, bringing out the post for all the students, they gave us a black turkey, there were no white turkeys then; the black ones are called bronze turkeys now.' There weren't a lot of presents then although Charlie remembers getting a golliwog one year and a train another, that went round and round in circles. Then, one year, he had a great idea – he would catch Father Christmas in the act. 'I waited and waited ... but nobody ever came and I got no present that Christmas!'

There was no electricity in their house so the children took candles up to bed, and one night his sister Pauline set her hair alight and had to be rescued. Later, she worked in the post office before going on to do nursing in Charing Cross in England. 'Then she started to bring home Christmas decorations, until then we'd only had holly but she brought home tinsel and shop-bought decorations.'

Fair Day and Billy Fairplay

The family had a very big garden and were almost self-sufficient in vegetables, growing 'cabbage, broccoli, onions – hanks of onions. There was no Chinese or Indian food served up back then!' But there were Indian people in Portarlington, 'They had exotic turbans and big cases full of knick-knacks. They came around on Fair Days, as did a man from Dublin, Billy Fairplay, who played tricks on the street for sixpences. The Protestants would be singing hymns and Billy Fairplay would be singing out too, "Too late, too late will be the cry, Billy Fairplay with the money will pass you by."'

The fair took place once a month, on a Friday. 'The girls always got a day off because on one Fair Day a girl was killed at the fair. We didn't get the day off, though. There was manure everywhere, that's as true as God. We loved the Fair Day, people making bargains and selling a cow or maybe two, with spits flying and hands clapping and all the rest of it.

'There were two Cash brothers used to come riding in on horses. Then there was the horse blocker, he'd come up and look at your horse and offer you so much and you'd bargain with him. He'd go away then and offer a bit more and then when the fair would be over and people would be going home, he'd make you a last-ditch offer. Then another man would step in and make his offer and it'd be accepted and the horse blocker would walk away and leave it to the other man who was offering a lesser price, to keep the price down. It was all orchestrated and planned.'

Army Days and Meeting Elsie

Charlie joined the Irish army during the Second World War. 'I had stayed in school because there was nothing else to do. Then I went up to the Curragh and joined the army. I was sent to Connolly Barracks where they taught us to be soldiers. I spent three years in the army. It was a bit boring at times because we didn't have that much to do. I was a wireless operator. But I enjoyed the camaraderie with the others. When I came out, there was still no work and, sure, once the war was over, we were all turfed out.'

Elsie Rafferty was the love of Charlie's life. The couple met in St Ultan's Hospital in Dublin where she was working. Charlie had gone to the hospital with one of his pals who was calling to see another nurse and he was introduced to Elsie along the way. The couple eventually married and had five children: Maebh, Siobhan, Una, Eilís and Colm.

The Bell-Ringer
Cyril Galbraith
Born 30 December 1923

In the spring of 2019, ninety-five-year-old Cyril Galbraith made the news headlines as Ireland's longest-serving campanologist, having spent eighty years as a bell-ringer. Taney parish in Dundrum, Dublin, where Cyril still rings the bells, celebrated his milestone by launching an annual bell-ringing competition in his honour, and the bell-ringers of Taney presented him with a commemorative cup. The same week, Dublin's Lord Mayor, Nial Ring, hosted a reception in the Mansion House for the city's bell-ringers from the five towers in the city: St Audoen's, John's Lane, Christchurch Cathedral, St Patrick's Cathedral and Taney parish.

Getting into Bell-Ringing
Cyril tells me that his bell-ringing began in St Mary's Cathedral in Limerick in 1939 when he

Cyril in Taney Church, Dundrum, 2019.

was fifteen. 'At that time, in between the wars, there was really nothing to do. There were four or five of us knocking around, we were teenagers and there wasn't even a car on the roads. We were looking for a distraction and someone suggested that we go down to St Mary's Cathedral and ask them would they train us how to ring the bells, and that's how it started.

'You could say that I met my wife, Anne Patricia Myles, through bell-ringing. She was training as a bell-ringer too, she was five years younger than me, in Villiers School as well but I didn't know her from school as she was so much younger. There were quite a few girls in the bell-ringing group, about twelve of us altogether.'

When Cyril first went to live in Dublin, he rang the bells in St Patrick's Cathedral, but each of the five bell towers in the city would take turns at ringing out on Sunday mornings for service. 'I had to give up ringing in St Patrick's because I couldn't manage the stairs, they nearly killed me. Taney is like a gallery, you go up a spiral staircase to the bells. I was always a heavy-bell-ringer, I would ring bells that weighed a couple of tonnes; I can't do that now though. I couldn't pull them out onto the balance. Once I got it swinging, there was no problem. The bells in Taney are set on an axle. There's a big wheel at the side with a groove on it, and there's a rope in it, and you pull the rope and the bell starts going up. Then when it gets up to the balance, you can let it go slightly over. There is a stay going down from the axle, a piece of timber that goes down, and it hits a board down below.'

But despite his prowess with the bells, Cyril says, 'I couldn't play a piano or anything like that, but I like music.' And campanology is a great way to see the world. 'I've rung bells in England, Australia, Jersey, you would be welcome in any tower. They'll say, "Are you a bell-ringer?" and you join in.'

Cyril says it's an ecumenical undertaking and bell-ringers often ring the bells in churches of other denominations. 'I rang the bells in John's Lane but I never got to do the Angelus. But I am so glad I got involved in bell-ringing, it has been a way of life for me.'

Rescuing Bells for the Millennium

Cyril was part of a group that rescued the eight bells from St George's Church in Hardwicke Place, Dublin. The bells had been presented to the church in 1828 by the architect who designed it, Francis Johnston. They even get a mention in *Ulysses*. The church can be seen from the Blooms' house in 7 Eccles Street and Bloom describes the sound of the bells at the end of the 'Calypso' chapter: 'A creak and a dark whirr in the air high up. The bells of George's church. They tolled the hour: loud dark iron.'

When the church closed in 1990, the building was sold but the bells were not included in the sale. They were dismantled and put into safe storage. The Taney team got together to raise the necessary funding of £64,000 to restore and install them in Taney. There were donations and subscriptions from parishioners and also from the government's Millennium Committee.

Their deadline was 31 December 1999. They were determined that the bells would ring in the third millennium in their new home. Cyril was appointed as the first ringing master and the countdown to the millennium began. More than a thousand people gathered in the church grounds to hear the bells peal in the new year. The rector, Canon Desmond Sinnamon, conducted a short service along with the curate, Rev. Bernadette Daly, and the parish priest of Dundrum, Fr Donal O'Doherty.

But Cyril also sees the threat to the bells posed by a dwindling church. 'Well, there are very few peals of bells around. At the moment in Dublin, there are only the five. There is a bell-ringing competition on Saturday up in Drogheda. I'm going to that. I'm not competing because they ring for ten minutes and that's too long for me. We've won several competitions as the Taney Bell Ringing Society.' Cyril's son David has followed in the family tradition and is also a senior bell-ringer in Taney.

Cyril was born in Barrington Street in Limerick where his father, Joe, was secretary of William Todd and Company Drapers. His mother, Elizabeth Jane Walsh, came from farming stock in Adare. 'They got married in 1916, right in the middle of the Rising.' The couple went on to have four children: two boys – Edward, the eldest and Cyril, the youngest of the family – and two girls, Dorothy and Pauline. But Edward died when he was only three years old. 'He was killed by a kick from a cow on the farm my mother was born on. As far as I can gather, they didn't have cow barns or milking machines or anything, and they brought them up a passageway and milked them out there beside the house, and I would say he walked right out behind.'

A School Exchange to Pre-War Germany

Cyril went to Villiers School in Limerick and, in 1938, when he was fifteen, the school joined up with High School in Dublin to bring pupils on a school exchange to Germany. This was a major undertaking and quite extraordinary given that Europe was gearing up for war at the time.

Incredibly, before I met Cyril I had interviewed Dorothy 'Dot' Bolster who also attended Villiers School and who also travelled on that school exchange to Germany. They remembered one another and have similar recollections of the long journey and of staying in a country where the wheels of war were beginning to turn.

'When we arrived in Dresden, we were picked up there by various families. I was billeted out with a lad in a multi-storey building. He was the only child in the family and I stayed with him for the month that I was there and we all met up every day and were taken to various places of interest.' And was Cyril conscious of the fact that war was about to break out? 'Oh for goodness sake, there were air-raid sirens going every night and bombers searching and everything. And the food was rationed. The lad I stayed with, Gotthard Kretzschemar was his name.

There were air-raid sirens going every night and bombers searching and everything. And the food was rationed.

'Gotthard was in the Hitler Youth. He had his uniform and everything. I never spoke to him about it. His father lost an arm in the First World War. I remember that, when I was coming home, the father said to me, "I have something for you, Cyril." He hardly spoke any English and do you know what he produced? Posters that the company he worked with had made and they were all of the English royal family. And I said, "Well, I'll take them but we have no connection with the royal family in Ireland."

'I was in contact with Gotthard right through the war. He finished up as an interpreter for the American forces but I don't know what he did during the war. He was brilliant. He was the same age as me and he could speak six languages. He came over to Ireland, as the second leg of the exchange in 1939, spent a month with me and went back in August, just days before the war started.' Cyril says the trip cost his father twenty pounds and another tenner for pocket money.

Early Career

Cyril left school after his Inter Cert and went to work in W.J. Shaw & Sons, one of the four bacon factories in Limerick at the time; the others were Matterson's, O'Mara's and Denny's. 'They're all gone now. I started as a clerk there and I stayed until 1946 and then I saw a job advertised for a manufacturers' agent in Dublin. I got the job as a rep. I stayed there about a year and a half. They were wholesalers and they had everything. They used to import things, they had Peek Freans biscuits, Van Houten's cocoa and polish and stains for hardware. The company was in Dublin, but I worked the south, from Limerick. It was a bit of fun really. No free biscuits, though, I never even saw the biscuits.'

The company had huge problems getting petrol for their cars in those years, so Cyril used to drive to Galway or wherever he had to go, then he'd travel back to Limerick by bus at the end of the week and return by bus to pick up his car on the Monday and resume the cycle.

Love and Marriage

It was around 1950 that Cyril started seriously dating his wife-to-be, Anne Patricia Myles. She had finished her nurse training in Taunton in Somerset along with four of her friends and she came back to Ireland. 'When I started travelling first of all, cars were very scarce and I was one of the only people who had a car, supplied by the company. They were all second-hand cars, bangers really. Anyway, I proposed to her out in Killaloe in County Clare, beside the lake. I drove out one night,

I had it planned, had the ring in my pocket and all, a five-star diamond. I proposed and she said, "Yes please." And then I had to go back and ask her father if it was okay. It *was* okay. I knew him very well.'

Cyril and Anne got married about a year later, in June 1951. And they had six children, first David, Robert and Eric. 'We were trying hard for

Cyril and Anne's wedding, June 1951.

a girl at this stage and we had our fourth boy, Peter. But then Heather Patricia arrived. And then Barbara. Two girls at the end. We were delighted when the girls came.'

Cyril says times were tough enough for young couples in those early years but he was lucky because when they were planning to get married, they did a deal with a builder and an architect. 'I knew herself and her husband, she was in school with us. So John Shannon, who was a friend from school, and I did a deal with an architect to design two semi-detached houses in Limerick.' And here's another coincidence because John Shannon was Dorothy Bolster's first husband.

'They started building in January. I would go away for a couple of nights and I would come back and there wouldn't be any progression. So I went to the builder and said, "Look, I want a date from you, I don't want to get married until the house is finished." And he said, "I promise the house for you in June." So we went ahead and booked the wedding for the thirtieth of June, gave him the whole month. Do you know when we got the house? October.'

Career Progress and a Move to Dublin

In the meantime, Cyril had joined Cooper, McDougall and Robertson. 'Three English chemists who started this veterinary supply company, and I worked with them from 1946 to 1950, and then we were taken over by the Wellcome Foundation. At that point, I had nearly half of Ireland to work, from Wexford to Donegal, everything west of that. I had a decent car then, an Austin.'

Cyril is very pleased with the improved road system since the days when he was travelling the country. 'I remember when I used to come to Dublin, it would take me as long to go from Naas to Dublin as it would Limerick to Naas because of all the fiddly little towns I had to pass through. The new roads are terrific and make travelling so much easier.'

And his views on politics? 'I was always a Fine Gael man but that's beside the point. I think Leo Varadkar is doing a good job. A lot of people don't, but I think he is doing a first-class job.'

When the company gave Cyril a big promotion in 1968 it meant a move, and Cyril had to find schools for all six children. 'The headmaster of Wesley was a clergyman called Gerald Myles, and he would be a first cousin of my father-in-law. And he married us. I was always telling people it was a mixed marriage. I was Church of Ireland and my wife was Methodist. So anyway we all had a laugh at that. Ger Myles used to come down to Limerick and he used to say to me, "When are you going to send the boys up to Wesley?" And I would say,

"Gerald, I couldn't afford it, with your fees and having to pay digs for them."

'Anyway, I was transferred to Dublin and the first thing I did was go in to see him. Wesley at that time was in Stephen's Green. I said, "I have great news for you, we're coming to live in Dublin." "Oh that's great," he said. "You haven't heard the good news yet," I told him. "Four of the boys will be coming to Wesley." And he looked at me and said, "Do you realise we have a four-year waiting list?" "Ah, you needn't worry," I replied, "my sister Pauline is a teacher and she'll get them into The High School." And he said, "Send them in in the morning!"'

Cyril finished his working life with Wellcome. 'I looked after the veterinary business. The powers that be in the UK, they got in touch with ICI, and they have a veterinary division too. And they said, over a few jars, "Aren't we stupid spending a few million a year looking after the same products? Why not get together?" So they decided that they would close all the Wellcome companies, and all the veterinary companies for ICI, and form a new company. They couldn't call it Wellcome or ICI, and the only internationally known name was Cooper's, so they went back to Cooper Animal Health.

Wellcome were one of the top manufacturers, one of the first companies to produce something that would kill a virus, Zovirax. They were the first people to do that.'

Life After Anne

Anne died in 1997 and Cyril says he misses her a lot. 'Oh I do, of course I do. I had retired at the time; if I was still working it might not have been so bad. She died in September. We used to go to Westport, bowling, first week in March and first week in October. She was a great indoor bowler. She was bowling on the Thursday before she died, and I went back bowling on the Tuesday and I went bell-ringing, and I used to do outdoor bowling, and I went to that. That helped. My children were all grown up then too.'

Some years ago Cyril was appointed glebe warden in the parish of Taney when they were building the parish centre. 'It meant I was in charge of the buildings and the people working there. You had to keep an eye out that they were doing it according to the specifications. One of the things I was responsible for was putting in the area for cremation urns. There was a plot there, a green plot, and we applied to the city council to get it as a site for urns, a garden of remembrance. We got permission, and it was up to me to get it done. This rector we had, Des Sinnamon, was the nicest man and a great administrator, but if you came up to him and said, "Do you see that plot over there, I think that would make a great—" "That's a great idea, Cyril," he would say. "You look after it." He was great at delegation!'

The garden of remembrance was installed in St Nahi's churchyard and Cyril paid £200 to have his own memorial space. His wife Anne's ashes have been interred there. 'We talked about cremation and we decided that that is what we wanted. There's a place there for me now.'

And then there is the future of religion itself. Does he think it is on the way out? 'Oh definitely,' he says. 'They were talking on the radio this morning about First Communion classes and the priest even said, "Are we wasting our time?" Basically what happens is – the kids are christened, confirmed, married and gone. I honestly think when my generation is gone, it will fizzle out.' However, he points out that Taney lays claim to the biggest Church of Ireland parish church in the twenty-six counties, supporting a healthy number of parishioners and with up to three hundred people still attending services every Sunday.

Does he describe himself as religious? 'To a degree. I'm a good Christian, I believe all the Christian principles and I go to church every Sunday.' And regarding death? 'I'm ready to go any time I'm called. I wouldn't mind. I feel as though I have had a good life, I've no complaints. Probably there's a lot of things that I didn't do, but otherwise ...'

And although Cyril believes in an afterlife, he doesn't think we'll meet the loved ones who have gone before us. 'No, I don't, to tell you the truth. I never bothered too much about it. I think there will be an afterlife, they say it will be better than the life we have now. It's hard to know.'

1924: Major Events

World

- Two US army planes complete the first round-the-world flight in 175 days

- The first Winter Olympics is held in Chamonix, France

- Ellis Island closes as an entry point for immigrants to the USA; the first immigrant to go through the process there in 1892 was Annie Moore from Ireland

- Jimmy Carter, Doris Day and Marlon Brando are born

Ireland

- Seán O'Casey's drama *Juno and the Paycock* opens at the Abbey Theatre

- Sinn Féin commemorates the anniversary of the events of the 1916 Easter Rising

- Dublin Corporation officially renames Sackville Street as O'Connell Street

- A new Licensing Bill is introduced by Minister for Justice Kevin O'Higgins. Pubs are allowed open between 9 a.m. and 10 p.m. and the sale of alcohol is limited to those over the age of eighteen

- Minister for Education Eoin MacNeill announces that the teaching of Irish is to be made compulsory in all schools

- The defence forces are established, incorporating the National Army

- Éamon de Valera is arrested at Newry Town Hall after defying an order preventing him from speaking in Northern Ireland

- All-Ireland champions: Dublin (hurling) and Kerry (football)

The Loveliest Butter

Dorothy Talbot
Born 13 February 1924

Dorothy 'Dot' Talbot grew up at 4 Alverna on the Mardyke with her parents, Isabelle Cassidy and Jack Talbot, who worked for Woodford Bourne, Grocers and Wine Merchants in Cork City. She had two siblings, Joan and Bertie. Dot's first memory is of being taken to a photographer – she still has the photo. 'That photo there is one of my first memories. I was an only child for four years and they brought me to a photographer and that picture was taken. I was a contrary little so and so in those days, always really, and there were books on the table and I wanted to look at those books, I didn't want to be bothered looking at a camera. I can remember that.'

Then, there was her fifth birthday. 'My mother stupidly put sweets up behind a clock and I had

Dot at four years old, 1928.

to have them and, when I got them, the clock came down as well. And I took to my heels: my grandmother lived across the road, and my mother came over like a tornado after me but my grandmother wouldn't let her touch me. Things like that happened. My grandmother was lovely, a lovely white-haired woman, and I lived with her for two years and we were the best of friends.'

Dot says she wasn't a 'dolly' person. 'I wanted a bike for my birthday when I was six but I got a doll and a pram. So what I did was, I walked the doll and the pram up the Mardyke and left them behind a tree, hoping that I might get my bike then. But, of course, instead of that I probably got a wallop.'

A Taste of the Country

The family regularly visited her aunt's farm in Tralee. 'We used to go back to the farm every year. My mother used to buy a pair of boys' shorts and a few blouses, and my sister and myself would go down to Kerry and we would stay there for a fortnight, and then my mum and my dad would come down in the car and we would all have a fortnight together. So we were there, living wild, absolutely enjoying it, riding ponies bareback, absolutely wonderful.

'I have a great liking for cream and I think it started there, because they had their own dairy. I used to be in under the separator, licking the cream. To this day, I have cream every day. I put it on my cereal in the morning. Strawberries at night. They also made their own lovely butter. I've never tasted anything as good, I've been looking for country butter all my life!'

Political Allegiance and a Move to Limerick

As a child Dot wasn't particularly conscious of the political tensions in the country. 'But I could kind of remember my father and mother talking about people that were involved. My mother had great stories of the Black and Tans because everyone had to be home by four o'clock – there was a curfew. They talked a lot about that. My mother had a job in Cork and they had to clear the streets by four o'clock and if you were caught out you were in terrible trouble. Then, of course, Cork was burned by the Black and Tans, but that was four years before I was born.

My mother had a job in Cork and
they had to clear the streets by four
o'clock and if you were caught out
you were in terrible trouble.

'I think my mother thought I was an IRA woman at one stage, I used to be very republican in my ideas. But with what goes on you wouldn't be long getting out of that. Juvenile ideas really.' However, Dot does admit to being influenced by the Big Fellow. 'We were always Fine Gael people, and I remember going to see the places associated with Michael Collins. But he died in the twenties so he was dead when I got interested in him.'

Dot attended a primary school in Sunday's Well. 'We used to have a beautiful walk up the Mardyke, through Fitzgerald Park, across the Shaky Bridge and up to Sunday's Well. It was a Protestant school. I remember enjoying it. We put on an operetta and my mother made dresses out of crepe paper. We had the writer David Marcus and his brother in the school and I think they would have written a lot of the stuff that went on in there. They were very talented even in those days. It was a mixed school, most Protestant schools were. I did my exam to get a scholarship to a secondary school and I got it and moved to a grammar school in Cork.'

Then Dot's parents were transferred to Limerick where her father was manager of a new branch of Woodford Bourne. 'They didn't know at the time if there was a decent secondary school in Limerick so I was left in Cork with my granny and grandfather. I really enjoyed it.' Dot played hockey and joined the Girl Guides.

Then, two years later, she moved to Limerick to be with her parents. She was enrolled at Villiers School on Henry Street which has now moved to the North Circular Road. The headmaster was Jerome Burrows, an extraordinary man who organised a student exchange with Germany on the eve of the

Second World War. 'In 1938 I was fourteen and four of us set off with the headmaster and his wife up to Dublin and met up with the school of boys that were going. I remember one of their teachers, he brought us all round the art galleries in Dublin before we left. The trip was overland, trains and boats. I remember the German trains had wooden seats and we missed the connection from Cologne to Dresden, which was our final destination. So we were seven hours in the railway station and I can remember these very wide windowsills in the station waiting room and myself and one of the other girls climbed up and slept head to toe on the windowsill. The headmaster slept on the floor, under the table.' Dot also remembers the towering view of Cologne cathedral from the windows of the station.

So we were seven hours in the railway station and I can remember these very wide windowsills in the station waiting room and myself and one of the other girls climbed up and slept head to toe on the windowsill. The headmaster slept on the floor, under the table.

Eventually they reached Dresden. 'All the parents were there to collect us. We were all staying with families, I was with this girl, an only child, in an apartment, four storeys up, on the main street in Dresden. And every night I could hear the German soldiers goose-stepping up the street. And every night her father disappeared, and I remember saying something to her about where he went. "Oh, he's working for Germany," she told me.

And every night I could hear the German soldiers goose-stepping up the street. And every night her father disappeared, and I remember saying something to her about where he went. 'Oh, he's working for Germany,' she told me.

'We were taken around various places; there were soldiers everywhere. I don't think I was frightened, but I didn't know what was going on anyway. One time they took us to an exhibition, an outdoor place, and I had a little camera with me.

And I remember there were these dreadful 'anti-Jew' signs. And I was just about to take a photo and she *grabbed* the camera from me. I probably would have been in trouble for taking photos.'

A few months later, the German students visited Ireland. 'I will never understand how they could allow children to come over to us in 1939. I always think that they never thought Hitler would go to war. The children all stayed with their exchange student. We were taking trips down to Killarney and all that, and she used to cycle with us. I will always remember my mother saying to me, "She's a real little Nazi." That was my mother all right!'

I will never understand how they could allow children to come over to us in 1939. I always think that they never thought Hitler would go to war.

Religious Segregation

A secretarial college followed. 'My headmaster wanted me to go to university but my parents wouldn't have been able to afford to send both me and my brother. And anyway, I had a boyfriend.'

The highlight of the social scene for teenagers then were the Protestant dances. 'This is the terrible segregation that went on in Ireland when I was young. We were in what was called the Men's Association. They had a hall in town that we played table tennis in and there were dances. There would be a band, you went and sat around.'

So everyone went? 'Yes,' says Dot's daughter, Valerie. 'Everyone – grannies and children and lovers in between. My mother used to do the catering. She loved baking, and there would be tea halfway through the dance and it was very social. It was a way of keeping the Protestants together because, once you married and had children, you were gone. It was very important that Protestants married Protestants in those years. We were diminishing.'

Dot illustrates this with the story of her own Aunt Louie who fell in love with a Catholic. 'I have great photos of them when they were young, cycling around Crosshaven, that was their place. They were always together. Anyway, one Friday evening, this had all been arranged, my aunt left work and went to the boat, went to England and married Jackie in England. A Catholic. He had a sister over there and she had it all set up. I can remember my grandmother didn't speak to that aunt for years. Dreadful days.'

Falling for John Shannon

Dot herself had met and fallen in love with John Shannon, a Protestant, when she was only seventeen. 'He was local and we were all involved in the same things. He was into scouting and I was into guiding, eventually I became the Girl Guide Commissioner. He was eight years older than me. I fell gradually in love with him.'

John asked Dot to marry him the following year. 'We were having a walk, we used to walk a lot. We stopped on a railway bridge and looked down and ... yeah! He asked me and I said yes.'

Dot's parents refused to let her marry until she was twenty-one but their wedding, in 1945, during the war years, proved difficult to organise. 'We had to get coupons for anything we needed to buy. My mother, we used to say, had "the leg of a fella" in Roches Stores and he used to help her out and get extra wool and things like that. Don't ask me where I got the material for the dress but it was a lovely hyacinth blue. A woman in Limerick made it.'

The couple got married in Trinity Church and

the wedding breakfast was at home. 'My mother was a great cook. I remember the morning of the wedding and the food ready for everyone.'

They went on honeymoon to Donegal. 'My husband had been on a great holiday up in Donegal and thought it would be a great idea to have the honeymoon there. We brought our bikes, because that's the only way you could get around Donegal. We put them onto the train in Limerick and the

Dot and John's wedding, 1945.

journey to Dublin took seven hours because they were running on turf at the time.

'We were staying in the Clarence Hotel along the quays for the night, and the next morning we got up and started off for Donegal. I still remember leaving my wedding in a suit and a large hat, and for some unknown reason I brought that bloody hat with me! Anyway, we set off on a bus, it went so far, then we had to get off and wait by the side of the road for another bus, and then the last bit, we had to cycle. We cycled all around Donegal. We stayed in Glencolmcille. We did a lot of cycling over the years so, later on, we got a tandem and we used to cycle down to Cork from Limerick and stay with my aunt.'

These were the years when women had to resign their job on marriage and Dot had been working with Ranks, the flour mills in Limerick. 'I was twenty-one and I had to retire. It was crazy, but it was a thing at the time. I was part-time. Before I went into Ranks, I was working in the Guinness office in Limerick. The barges would deliver the Guinness from Dublin.'

And when her husband became very ill with a chest complaint, Guinness' offered her part-time work. 'Rationing had come in and they had to keep track of the stout. So they employed me to be in charge of the rationing. I had to make sure people didn't get more than their quota. Everybody used to come in and order their stout and I would have to make sure they didn't get too much. That was in 1947.'

John was working with Matterson's Bacon plant at the time. 'They were terribly good to him, they gave him full pay and everything, but it was a worrying time. I remember saying to my mother, "I don't know how I'm going to make ends meet," and she said, "You have a spare room up there, why don't you take in two girls, they'd be delighted to have a place and they can work in Shannon." So that's what I did, we bought two single beds and put them in the front room and brought in two girls. They were lovely girls, great fun.'

Then Dot's children arrived and she took the unusual step of naming them after famous authors. 'Whoever I was reading at the time,' she says. When she had her first child Mort, Dot recalls the maternity services of the time. 'I was three and a half weeks early and I thought I'd better get back in to the nursing home, it doesn't look good. It was St Benedict's Nursing Home in Limerick. They kept me in and gave me some sedative early in the morning and it put me out and next thing I woke to some woman roaring and screaming and shouting in the next room. I was damned if I was going to scream and shout. But, eventually, I knew there was something happening that shouldn't be happening and I roared and a nurse came in and whisked me away and they had an operating table there, so he was born five pounds, very small.'

After Mort came two girls, Karen and Valerie. 'One day – Mort was about six, he was in school, and I had the two little ones at home, we lived on the North Circular Road – a milk cart came along and Valerie put Karen up on top of it for their little jaunt. I was inside thinking they were just playing in the garden, and the next thing they were gone, no sign of them anywhere, and someone said, "I think they were on that milk cart." Valerie was very young at the time and she thought the cart would be coming back again because it was a circular road but he had done his circle and he was off again wherever he was going next.'

'He Dropped Dead Up There'

John retired in 1982. 'He was hale and hearty, as we thought. The sergeant here had an elderly father and he used to come down to us, and John had his boots in the car and he used to take him up to the golf course and they'd have nine holes and be back. And this particular morning I said I'd have a great day in the garden and the two of them went off and about an hour and a half later, in the front door walked the old man, the sergeant's father. "What are you doing here?" I said. "Where's John?"

'"Ah, he's gone," was the reply. Now he was very old, and I said, "Gone where?" And he said, "He dropped dead up there." I wouldn't mind so much but he said, "He had a great shot up onto the green before he died."

So Dot tore up to the golf club. 'And fair enough, they had the priest, and the doctor had been, and he was there laid out with his head on his golf bag. He was seventy-two. And very active.'

Rationing was a way of life in the early years of marriage. 'It was pretty tough. I always remember we were terribly lucky in the way that my father came from the country and the aunt that we used to go down to as kids, they had their own dairy.'

As was common at the time, members of Dot's family had joined the British army. There is a photo of a Kerry uncle in uniform who later emigrated to New Zealand. He signed up when he was sixteen and became a despatcher in Russia. 'It was long before me but, in Ireland, on the farms, the eldest boy gets everything and the others have to fend for themselves and find something to do, and he was the youngest.'

Dot's brother Bertie is a Church of Ireland minister and she remembers that the family always went to church on a Sunday. 'I went to Sunday school and, of course, at one stage of my life, I was terribly religious.' Until February 2019, Dot was the church warden in her local Church of Ireland in Spanish Point. It's a small church where her duties included looking after the silver, opening up the church and making sure everything was ready for services.

Dot believes in the afterlife. 'I hope they're not too hard on me. I do. That's our Christian faith. I definitely feel there is a God. He's just being hard done by at the moment.'

She would describe herself as 'liberal'. She voted yes to same-sex marriage and to abortion. 'I think they were good decisions, they did an awful lot of good for people. I like Ireland at the moment.'

Second Marriage

Two years after John Shannon died, Dot married Robin Bolster, who had been a long-time family friend. The whole family used to play cards together and knew one another well. Dot and her family had spent many happy summers in a caravan in Spanish Point, the coastal village in County Clare where she now lives. 'We went to Roundstone for a fortnight, that was our family holiday, and then back here. The two girls and myself would stay here and teach ourselves to crochet. We caravanned everywhere for years and years. We were saying when my husband retired that we would buy a house down here.'

In the meantime, Robin had bought a house in Spanish Point. 'But it was a wreck, there were notices on the window – "Please do not open this window" – probably because it would fall apart. I remember my father coming down and saying, "That man must be mad." Nevertheless, John and Dot bought half the house from Robin. Then, in 1988, John died and, two years later, Dot and Robin married.

Robin died in 2008 and Dot still lives in the same house in Spanish Point.

Dot still plays golf and drives, and she can remember the registration of her first car – BTI 243. Each year, she goes on holiday to Lanzarote with her two daughters. She now has five grandchildren and two great-grandchildren. She is an avid reader. 'I love reading. I read an awful lot. I have a Kindle now because you can increase the font, my eyes aren't great. I love Diana Gabaldon, the author of the Outlander books. That series is wonderful. I hope I'm still alive next year because her last book of the series is due out then.'

Dot has just one piece of advice for young people today. 'Have a good life and follow your dreams.'

Civil War and Heartbreak

Marie Elliott
Born 3 October 1924

'I can remember my mother sitting on the swing with my sister Pat on her knee. Pat was less than a year old, so I was about three and a half, that's one of my earliest memory.'

Marie Curran and her family had moved from Dublin to Westport where her father, who was an accountant, worked as a local government auditor. 'He was a young man at the time, of course, and he was sent to Westport for two years to work, so we moved the whole family to Westport.' Although his office was in Castlebar, they couldn't find a house there, so they lived in Westport and he commuted.

Joseph Curran was the father of Marie and Pat, and Aileen O'Neill was their mother. Marie recalls her father getting a car. 'He was friendly with an older doctor who had bought this brand-new car, but he couldn't manage it and, after a week, he wanted to get rid of it, and my father bought it, probably for buttons. My father had never driven a car before. It was a Mathis, a French car, and I remember the number – IX 579. You had to step up onto the running board to get in. I remember being in the car on the way to Westport, and the car was full of luggage. I was about three.'

Another memory from Westport was of the time her father made a kite for a little boy who lived nearby. 'A kite in those days was a great treat, forerunner of all these drones now, if you got the wind. My father made this kite for this little boy, and I remember holding the kite and it lifted me over the ground. I clearly remember being lifted off the ground and Daddy rushing to grab me.

'Another thing I remember, my parents loved fish, but they couldn't buy fish in Westport. There was a fish shop on D'Olier Street in Dublin called Sawers and they put a pound of plaice on the train every Thursday night and it cost a pound and sixpence, and it was delivered to my mother in Westport. Imagine, you couldn't buy fish in Westport!'

Marie and her sister Pat.

Teddy in the Attic

Marie went to school for the first time when they lived in Westport. 'I think it was to get me out of the way, but I loved it. Apparently at this one-room school in Westport, everybody was bigger than me and made a big fuss of me. One little boy went home and said that there was a new girl in his class, and she had rosy cheeks and a Paris accent. They never knew where he got that from.'

When Marie was three she was given a Teddy bear. 'I still have him, he's up in the attic, but he's moth-eaten and the straw is coming out of him. I love that teddy.'

But there were less happy memories of childhood too. When she was five, she contracted scarlet fever. 'I didn't have to go to hospital. I can remember, my father sat up every night with me, he slept in a chair in the bedroom with me. I think it took six weeks or something, in those days. It was one of those big wicker chairs, like an armchair and, to this day, I can hear the creak of that at night when he slept in that chair. He was wonderful with kids.'

Life in Muckross Park

'When we came back to Dublin, I was sent to Muckross Park in Donnybrook, and I tore the house down. I started there in 1929 and I was only five. There were a hundred pupils in the whole school and that included the boarders.'

Marie has vivid memories of her time in Muckross. 'There was Miss Peggy Randall, she was the Montessori teacher. When I was in sixth, there was only seven of us in the class and all of us had started in babies. Mona McGregor, Pearl Dunne, Nancy Healy, Pat Maugham, Betty O'Donoghue, Maureen Lemass and me. I first met Maureen [who would marry Charles Haughey] at a dancing class in Wicklow Street, and the teacher was Maureen Traynor. We were only four years old then.

'Maureen had a very flat voice in those years and one of the nuns, Sr Bernadette, used to say to her that some day her father, Seán Lemass, could be leading the country and he couldn't have a daughter speaking like that. The funny thing is, her sisters Peggy and Sheila didn't have that accent.'

Marie's class kept in touch long after they left school and a past pupil, Judy Lyons, organised a reunion party when they were all eighty years old. 'I came home and my two granddaughters were here and I nearly had to pick them up off the floor – they were roaring laughing at the idea of us going to a school reunion at that age. But sure now I am ninety-four. You see, Muckross was so small that you knew everybody and you knew their families, you knew their children, you even knew where they lived.'

'I Would Hear My Father Talking'

The 1920s were turbulent times in Ireland. 'I would hear my father talking, he was a great admirer of Michael Collins, he spent thirteen months in Ballykinlar [an internment camp during the War of Independence], almost by mistake, but he was there. It was a terrible place. He always said that the Civil War broke his heart. That families turned on each other.

Marie and Pat with their parents.

'He was also terribly worried about Hitler and Germany. He could see trouble coming. He had just lived through the First World War, then the Civil War, and it was only twenty years before the Second World War. It was terribly close. He was always saying that he thought he lived in the most exciting time in history. He saw the beginning of the car, the beginning of air travel and, what would be the third thing? The two world wars.

'He told us that, around 1916, he was up in the mountains, training with hurley sticks, marching up and down and, of course, they were arrested.

His father asked him about it. "Joe, you hadn't anything to do with this, had you?" And my father said, "Well, actually ..." Ironically, many years later, my father became the manager of the Royal Insurance Company, an English company.'

In the aftermath of Bloody Sunday in November 1920, there were wide-scale arrests. 'The following day, they rounded up everybody, any name they had, and my father was one of them. He ended up in Ballykinlar, and it was a terrible place by all accounts.

'When I was a bit older, there were a couple of general elections and I remember the excitement. My father was terribly disgusted with the way things turned out. He was a very strong supporter of Collins, which meant he was very anti-Dev. I was twenty-one when I first voted and I remember my father saying to me the night before, "Come here, now", and he drew out a voting paper and he showed me how to vote. "You fill every line, don't leave any blanks, and the person you like least you put at the bottom."'

The Eucharistic Congress and Summers in Kerry

The Eucharistic Congress in 1932 also created great excitement for the then seven-year-old. 'I had made my First Holy Communion the same year and we went to the children's mass in Phoenix Park. You couldn't take a car, all the roads were closed. My father and mother went twice because they wanted to hear John McCormack sing. He sang at the midnight mass I think, and all the trams were free.

'And there I was in my Communion dress, the second time I got to wear it. To a child, there seemed to be millions of people. I remember getting on the tram opposite McBirney's on Aston Quay. There was a tram there that went to the park. It must have gone up the quays. It was so exciting, I couldn't sleep for weeks leading up to it and for weeks after it, thinking about it. My parents were with me, it was a huge thing, people came from all over the world.'

During the thirties, the family went on summer holidays to Kerry. 'We would go for a month and Pat and I would cry all the way home. We loved it. We stayed in Templemore House, a farmhouse, situated between Kenmare and Parknasilla. It was lovely. I went back there years later and even the stones on the road hadn't changed. There was one little harbour, a little pier, and that is where I learned to dive, when the tide was in. Once my father dived in and lost his swimming trunks and we all had to be ushered away while my mother got a towel.'

But then the war came and they couldn't travel to Kerry anymore because they couldn't get enough petrol for the car. 'There were no cars on the road for five or six years. But the next thing I heard, we were going to Bettystown for holidays. Imagine! My mother and father were both golfers and no matter where we went, we had to be near a golf course. There was a train to Bettystown and I remember we had the cat with us and the cat got out of the box in Amiens Street Station and climbed away up into the roof and they had to get her down. They were both animal lovers. It was so funny.'

Love at the Hop

But Bettystown had great significance for Marie. 'That's where I met my future husband, Neil, at the hop. We were staying in the Northlands Hotel.

I was sixteen, I was still at school when I met Neil.' But was it love at first sight? 'No, not at all. I got to know him then though, and I was only allowed go to the hop during school holidays. He lived in Dublin too, he was just on holidays.'

Winters were colder when Marie was young. 'Every winter, we were togged out, we got a new winter coat and we got one Sunday dress, a good dress that you wore for occasions, and about three skirts and lots of jumpers. And liberty bodices. There was underwear, chill-proof, and a liberty bodice was like a little sleeveless jacket that went on over the vest to keep you from getting pneumonia. The cold was something else. During the war, we only had one warm room, when nobody could get coal.'

Wartime in Ireland

After her Leaving Certificate, Marie did a secretarial course and then she got a job in the Bank of Ireland in College Green. Working in the bank on the last day of the Second World War gave her a unique view of the VE Day attack on Trinity College. It started when a group of students celebrated by decorating the college with Union Jacks. Students from University College Dublin retaliated. 'We were allowed up onto the roof, there was a huge roof, of course. There was a terrible attack on Trinity College ... crowds ... like a riot. It went on all day. Why Trinity, I don't know. And this was the end of the war. It was like a mob, a rabble.'

Marie was meeting Neil. 'He was waiting for me. In the bank, we only had a half hour for lunch and we had to eat in the canteen. But we finished at half past four and I came out with Neil and walked up D'Olier Street and there was a baton charge, and I certainly wouldn't recommend being caught up in that! I remember Neil pushing me into a doorway, and the crowds surging along, and the police with batons.'

And VE Day celebrations? 'Relief I would say was the main reaction, relief that it was all over. We weren't in the war, thank God. That's one thing Dev did, I suppose. This is the 'Michael Collins' coming out in me when I say that!'

There was a dress code in the bank. 'We had to wear stockings and I made friends with a very cranky shop lady and she used to keep two pairs of stockings for me every month. It was hard to get them – this was during the war – and they were nine and tenpence for the two pairs. In the summer, we used to buy liquid makeup for our legs to make them brown. Like the fake-tan stuff now, leg makeup. And I remember my mother would say, "Wash your legs before you go to bed," because it would come off on the sheets. There was also a shop where you could have ladders repaired. It was down just opposite the Pro-Cathedral and you could get ladders mended for a shilling. It was hard to buy stockings. But it wasn't a question of money; we had the coupons and they had to do for a year, for shoes, clothes, anything.'

Things were still very hard to come by after the war. 'I remember my father wanted to give me a gold watch for my twenty-first birthday. But you couldn't buy gold watches, they weren't available. And, in the end, I got the gold watch the same day I got my engagement ring. And Pat, my sister, she was twenty-one and got her gold watch as well.

'Pat died of lung cancer, she was a heavy smoker. She would come to visit me and her breakfast consisted of a large cup of coffee and ten cigarettes. The house smelled like the top of a bus afterwards.' Marie used to be a smoker too but stopped after a spell in hospital when she wasn't allowed smoke. 'But I didn't miss it. When I came home I didn't want to smoke and I never smoked again. It gave me up.'

Headgear was a big thing then. 'All the ladies who would come to our house in my childhood for tea, they always wore their hats. They would never take their hats off, they would take their coats off.' And buying a hat was a big adventure. 'I can remember going with my mother and spending hours choosing a hat in Clerys. There was also a very good hat shop called Mensey's, down opposite Arnotts in Henry Street. My friend Nuala bought a hat there one day and they had lovely bags with a string at the top to carry the hat. And when she got to the bus stop she looked down and she had the string but no hat. Somebody had cut it. And that is a long time ago.'

Babies in the Fifties

Later, there was the birth of her two daughters and she was attended privately by Dr Arthur Barry. 'I went to see him every month. The bill, I think, was twenty-five guineas for all the treatment. I had the babies in Stella Maris, which was in Earlsfort Terrace, almost directly opposite the university. There were only eight rooms. I remember when Aileen was born on the twenty-ninth of December.

And because of the date she was born, it technically made her a year older when she was two days old. I remember the bells ringing in Christchurch on New Year's Eve, and I remember saying to Neil, "I'm never going to stay in again on New Year's Eve." But the nursing home was like a first-class hotel. For two weeks. They wouldn't let you take the baby home for the first two weeks because you wouldn't get a night's sleep.'

Marie also tells the story of her cousin, Noreen, an extraordinary woman who adopted three children and who insisted on getting the names and addresses of all three mothers. 'The authorities didn't want to give them to her, so she had mass said for those mothers on each of the birthdays. Noreen died and the children stayed together and looked after their father. I don't know if they tracked down their mothers. One of them asked when she was about seven, "Why couldn't I have grown in your tummy, Mummy?" Anyway Noreen explained that there was "something broken" in her tummy, but that it didn't matter. And the little one said, "Well, I don't want any other mummy."

'They waited about six or seven years after adopting the first child before getting the second one, and then they got a third about eighteen months after that. When they were waiting for the second child, little Ailbhe said, "When are we going to get the baby, Mummy?" Noreen explained that their babies were very special and that's why they had to wait, to which Ailbhe replied, "Ah don't bother, just get me a normal one."'

Mistaken Identity

Trams were the main mode of transport in Dublin in the fifties and Marie tells a story about her father-in-law, Maurice Elliott, who was in town one evening. 'All the trams stopped at Nelson's Pillar. There was the fifteen that went out by Rathgar, and the seven and the eight went to Dalkey. But the trams were all in the same space. Maurice was standing in the Rathgar queue, and he looked over and saw a neighbour of his family, but he was in the wrong queue, he was in the Dalkey one. So Maurice went over, the neighbour was a bit under the weather. So he went and got him and put him in the right tram and they got out at the right stop, he only lived a few houses over. So Maurice, being very kind, helped him up the step and rang the doorbell. The man of the house himself opened the door, and he was the image of the man that Maurice had "rescued"! So what did he do? He brought him back, put him on the next tram going into town and paid his fare, and hoped that when he got to the Pillar, he would get out and get into his own tram home!'

Religious Views

So, how has Ireland changed over Marie's lifetime?

'I think it has changed utterly. Not all for the best. I look back and wonder what kind of fools we were to listen to John Charles McQuaid, who could come into the school and stop us playing hockey against Protestant schools. That actually happened in Muckross. He stopped all girls' Catholic schools from associating with Protestant schools. We used to play every Saturday, I was a keen hockey player and I was always on the team, and every Saturday we would have a friendly. They would come to us on a Saturday afternoon and we had to stop that, and we had won the cup the previous year.

> I look back and wonder what kind
> of fools we were to listen to John
> Charles McQuaid, who could come
> into the school and stop
> us playing hockey against
> Protestant schools.

'I just couldn't believe in limbo either. I always tell the story about going down to the village; naturally we didn't have fridges or freezers and we shopped every day. We had a safe outside the door for the milk. [A safe was an outdoor cupboard, made of wood and the sides were metal with hundreds of tiny holes through which air could pass but insects were unable to enter. It kept the food cool and insects out.] I remember a lady I used to meet shopping. Her husband died and she was terribly stressed and I was trying to console her, and she said, "I am very annoyed. Father so and so told me that my husband would be in purgatory for a fortnight." How would he know that? She was so upset. Like, whoever came back to tell that priest?'

Marie does believe in an afterlife and feels that loved ones who have died are still close to us. 'I appreciate my mother more since she died. She was a character, really, she played golf and bridge. And that was another thing, we had no television and no radio yet. My parents played a lot of house bridge in particular. Various couples would come and have supper and play bridge and my parents would go to their house. It put me off, I don't like cards. They tried to get me to learn bridge, but I couldn't get the hang of it at all. And the funny thing is they would say, "You should be good at it, you're good at mathematics." I have a strong memory for numbers. I remember phone numbers of people who are dead. That's useful!'

1925: Major Events

World

- Benito Mussolini assumes power in Italy as dictator

- 40,000 members of the Ku Klux Klan hold a rally in Washington DC

- The first television transmitter is built by John Logie Baird

- F. Scott Fitzgerald's *The Great Gatsby* is published in the USA

- Field Marshal Hindenburg is elected president of Germany and Adolf Hitler publishes *Mein Kampf*

- Margaret Thatcher and Richard Burton are born

Ireland

- The Dublin Metropolitan Police merges with the Civic Guard, the new organisation to be known as An Garda Síochána

- Alexander Hull & Co., building contractors, are to rebuild the General Post Office, Dublin at a cost of £50,000

- Annie Walsh becomes the last woman to be executed in Ireland, for the murder of her husband

- Tuam Workhouse becomes the Bon Secours Mother and Baby Home

- Liam O'Flaherty's novel *The Informer*, set in Dublin in the aftermath of the Civil War, is published

- All-Ireland champions: Tipperary (hurling) and Galway (football)

A Fair Day to Remember

John Flanagan
Born 28 February 1925

In the 1870s, Paddy Flanagan left his home in the border area between Ballyconnell in County Cavan and Ballinamore in County Leitrim to travel to Alaska. Though Paddy had married Annie Kiernan from Aughavas in County Leitrim in 1918 before he left for Alaska, and had had a daughter, his son John Cormac Flanagan, was born after he returned home to Ireland. John remembers the talk around his father. 'He went to America at sixteen. He died in 1930 when I was only five. Most people travelled to Scotland from Leitrim so this was a big trip. He was in Alaska during the Gold Rush. He was diabetic and he was one of the first in Ireland to be treated with insulin, it was only discovered in 1922. My father didn't work much when he got the diabetes. He had to weigh food and all the rest.

He had to get beef and other meat. I'm diabetic now and it is much easier.'

John's father had been living in America for nearly twenty years and sending money home to his own father, Micky Flanagan, to build a house. 'My sister was five years older than me, she was born in 1920 and I think there was another sibling that died at birth.'

'The Pain Was Terrible'

When John was twelve he was diagnosed with a disease of the bone and had to spend three months in hospital. 'The pain was terrible. I had to be in hospital for twelve weeks over Christmas. The hospital was forty-five miles away in Manorhamilton, at the other end of the county. My father was dead by then. I was brought to the hospital on my own by the ambulance, it was tough. I didn't see any of my family over Christmas and into January.

'There were three wards. One had five beds, that was a better ward. The middle ward had twelve beds and that is where I was. There were old men in it and six people died while I was there. One of them was in the bed next to me, I remember the prayers the nuns said, all the candles. I could touch the bed where he was dead next to me. It was very lonely. It was an old hospital, I was glad to get home.'

'We Couldn't Sell the Cattle'

John grew up on a farm. 'My young days were tough. You see, it was the Economic War [a retaliatory trade war between the UK and the Irish Free State that continued until 1938]. When my father died, he had the farm, forty-eight acres.' His mother then ran the farm on her own after her husband's death. 'We had all these cattle. I remember going to fairs and we couldn't sell the cattle. Calves were only five shillings, and they couldn't sell them, so they slaughtered the calves. Britain wouldn't take anything from us. This started in 1932.

We had all these cattle. I remember going to fairs and we couldn't sell the cattle. Calves were only five shillings, and they couldn't sell them, so they slaughtered the calves. Britain wouldn't take anything from us. This started in 1932.

'I remember as children, going to the fairs with six or ten cattle, and we would maybe sell one or two. We would walk them to Ballyconnell, which was over six miles away. We would start out at four or five in the morning. My mother did the buying and the selling. I remember herding the cattle at the Square, near the public house in Ballyconnell.'

But when it looked like war, John's mother took her own precautions. 'She bought half a tonne of flour, and she had more tea, in biscuit boxes. She bought it before the war, before it was rationed. And we had it in a room over the kitchen, so we had white bread until near the end of the war, it was all brown bread at the time. She baked, did all the baking. And we had our own food from the farm. We didn't do too badly.'

John left school at sixteen. 'I went to serve my time as a motor mechanic in Carron's garage in Ballinamore. I liked it, but it was during the war years and there were very few private cars on the road, there were only hackney cars. Three people had hackney cars in the town. The only other cars were owned by the priest and the doctor, so there wasn't much business. What I was doing was serving petrol really. When I went to the garage I had no wages, my mother had to pay twenty pounds for me to serve my time. It was supposed to take me three years until I was twenty. And all I was doing was fixing punctures and serving petrol. So after my apprenticeship, I did hackney work in Offaly.'

Then John got a job with the Automobile Association, on patrol. 'And everyone saluted me. It was a feature of the time that AA officers saluted any car bearing an AA membership badge.'

John Flanagan as a young man

Working on the Border

In the fifties, he was sent to Carrickarnon, a customs post on the border with Northern Ireland. 'You couldn't drive into Northern Ireland without a pass on the car. They were known as bonds but the AA used to issue a pass, known as a triptych. It guaranteed that you would take the car back from Northern Ireland. My job was to check the numbers of these cars with the triptych, and get Customs to stamp it. I was sixteen years there.'

But they were troublesome times on and near the border. John remembers the 1957 incident when Seán South and Fergal O'Hanlon, members of the IRA, were fatally wounded in a raid on an RUC barracks on New Year's Day. In November 1957, a landmine exploded prematurely in Edentubber, killing four republicans – Oliver Craven, Paul Smith, George Keegan and Patrick Parle – now known as 'the Edentubber Martyrs'. The owner of the house where they were preparing the landmine was also killed.

Smuggling

John has seen the parade of smuggling across the border go in both directions as economic circumstances have changed over the years. 'When I started, the buses from Northern Ireland used to come through, nearly one hundred buses a day at the weekend. This was after the war. The people from the North went to Dublin and Dundalk and Blackrock to do their shopping. They couldn't get nylons and stuff like that in the North; things were rationed in Britain. They had no butter, they would come down here and buy the butter in Dundalk. But Customs would take the butter off them if they were caught.'

But then the smuggling changed direction. 'About two years afterward, it all changed. They wouldn't take our butter then. And it was costing five shillings to produce it, and we were exporting it for two shillings a pound. So they were buying the Irish butter from us here, and taking it into the North, and smuggling it back down, and it was worth half a crown here. So it was worth smuggling. And they got away with it.'

John would prefer to see Britain remain in the EU. 'But if they leave, no matter what they say, we will have to have border posts.'

Marrying 'Miss Louth'

John met his wife, Elizabeth (Betty) Dorrian, in Dundalk. 'It was at a dance in the town hall. She was a good-looker. She had won the title of 'Miss Louth'. We were going out two or three years when I proposed to her.'

Does Betty remember the proposal? 'He usually claims it was *me* that proposed. I'm sure he did propose. You didn't get down on one knee anyway, that I do know!'

Miss Louth: Betty Dorian, John's wife.

So where did you get engaged? 'It was at home in the house, I think,' Betty says. 'Imagine, I forget an important thing like that!'

They married on 26 September 1956. The wedding was in Kilsaran and the reception was in the Ballymascanlon Hotel. 'There were over a hundred guests,' says Betty. 'Not that big now, but big back then.'

'We went on our honeymoon in Ireland,' John adds. 'I had a car at the time but it wasn't great so I hired one. We drove from Dublin. We couldn't go to Cork because there was a polio epidemic, and we were told not to go there.'

I had a car at the time but it wasn't great so I hired one. We drove from Dublin. We couldn't go to Cork because there was a polio epidemic, and we were told not to go there.

After they married, the couple settled in Castlebellingham. 'In a flat, and I was still working with the AA. We have two children, a boy and a girl. Linda is the eldest. She is retired now, but she was a social worker. And then the boy is Patrick. I ended up with a filling station, a garage, we still have it and he is still running it.'

But things changed on the border. The triptych was gone and John was made redundant there so he was offered a job in the AA radio room in Dublin, answering emergency calls for breakdowns. The couple already had a business by then. 'My wife worked in the drapery. She started a children's shop, a small little shop in Dundalk. We built a house at Dowdall Hill outside the town, and we only lived in it a couple of years when I was made redundant and was offered the job in Dublin. We intended to go but then she wasn't keen to move and I wasn't keen either. So I was commuting from Castlebellingham to Dublin, which was a bit unusual back then.'

Is he a religious man? 'I was ... more so than I am now. I still go to mass and, yes, I believe in an afterlife. I think when you get older you begin to wonder, *What if there is nothing there?* But there has to be something there.'

John Flanagan died on 19 July 2019. May he rest in peace.

A Missionary Life
Sr Cosmas Cullen
Born 19 November 1925

Sister Cosmas Cullen was born in Harold's Cross in Dublin but grew up in Churchtown which was then well outside the city limits. 'It was opposite the golf course, very country. There were no buses in those days and we had horses and carts. The post was delivered by a horse and van every day, and the milk was delivered every morning. It was lovely.'

> There were no buses in those days
> and we had horses and carts. The
> post was delivered by a horse and
> van every day and the milk was
> delivered every morning.
> It was lovely.'

She is the daughter of Mary Cullen, a midwife, and Patrick Bernard Cullen who was a traveller for Terry's Chocolate. There were eight children, four boys and four girls, and Sr Cosmas was the third eldest. Today, she is the only one still alive.

She describes an idyllic life. 'We were at the bottom of the Dublin Mountains, walking distance from the hills. The boys used to be caddies on the golf course and find balls and had great fun. They made a great living and they learned a great lot of golf, they all became great golfers.'

Gravitating Towards Australia

But then the family started to gravitate towards Australia, starting with her brother Desmond who emigrated when he was still a teenager. Then Paddy went, and Vincent and then Deirdre and her husband. 'Then when my mother died, my father went to visit Australia and he never came home. He said, "I'll spend a couple of years going around", but he loved it and he never came back. When I was eventually allowed to take my home leave, there was no point in coming back to Ireland because there was nobody left here.'

Life as a Franciscan Missionary

When Sr Cosmas was eighteen she joined the Franciscans at their mother house, Mount Oliver in Dundalk. 'It was the only house they had in Ireland. I was there for six months and then I went to the UK and did teacher training in London. Then I went to Africa. Once you entered the convent, time didn't mean anything. I just wanted to go on the missions and I was sent to Nkokonjeru in Uganda. It means 'The White Hen'.

'It was quite a busy place. That's where the African Sisterhood started. I was in charge of the vernacular teacher-training centre there. There was a primary class, for children aged five and six, and then a primary from one to four. That's the class I taught because they learned in their own language.'

Sr Cosmas had no knowledge of the language when she first arrived but says she learned it on the spot by teaching it. 'The language was Luganda. The people were Baganda. It wasn't a difficult language, as languages go. It's what they call an agglutinative language. You've a root, and then they add bits to the root. What would be a sentence in English would just be one word in Luganda.'

She recalls the culture shock when she arrived there. 'Well, I had never seen a black person in my life. I remember looking at them and being amazed. One day, I was going up the country somewhere and there was an African woman with her baby, he was only eight or nine months old, and he was crying.

So I took him up and he stopped crying and he gazed up at me and the little hand went up to my white face and he looked at it and you could see him wondering, *Does the white come off?* It was pretty much what I was wondering too.'

> The little hand went up to my white
> face and he looked at it and you
> could see him wondering, *Does the*
> *white come off?*

The area Sr Cosmas worked in was extremely poor. 'They had nothing. But they were very happy because they didn't know they were poor. Everybody was in the same condition. They lived very simply, very happily.'

In those days, missionaries didn't come home. 'We weren't allowed to come home, even for the death of a parent. But you accepted it, it was how things were and you knew this from the start. Everyone went through it.'

Then after twelve years, she was allowed a trip back. 'The pope had decided that missionaries should come home, for the sake of the parents if nothing else. That was 1962. By then, my mother had died. And that is a great sorrow to me because I never related to her as an adult. She died when she was sixty-two. She was diabetic and, in those days, they didn't have the medication they have now.'

> We weren't allowed to come home,
> even for the death of a parent. But
> you accepted it, it was how things
> were and you knew this from the
> start. Everyone went through it.

After her visit home, Sr Cosmos moved to work in Kenya and remained on the missions until she retired three years ago. 'I was working till then but not full-time. I retired from formal teaching at a secondary school, teaching A'Levels, and then I went into nursery teaching because I was convinced that the first year of a child's teaching is the most important. The attitude towards learning is formed then. To know that it is normal and natural and enjoyable. It's easy, it comes naturally, the brain is meant to learn, and I wanted children to realise that they're not being asked to do anything difficult.'

And although there were other visits home, Sr Cosmas chose to take her leave in Australia where most of her family were now living. 'I mostly stayed with my sister in Perth, Western Australia, but I did visit them all. It was wonderful, it is a beautiful country.' But she couldn't retire there as the Franciscans don't have a convent in Australia. All of their work is in Africa so she is now living in the Mount Oliver Convent in Dundalk, where there are twenty-five nuns resident. 'They're all like myself, we can't be on the missions because we are old or sick or whatever.'

She admits to being a bit lonely sometimes. 'All of my family are gone. Well, I have nieces and nephews and cousins and I love them and they're very good but it's not quite the same as having immediate family.' But she says that time passes very quickly. 'I can do what I like now. I find the time goes very fast. Just living takes so much time, trying to look after myself. But I am always happy, no matter where I am.'

'The Country Seems To Have Lost Its Soul'

And what of the Ireland Sr Cosmas has returned to, an Ireland she hadn't lived in for almost seventy years? 'It has changed greatly. The country seems to have lost its soul as far as I can see. For example,

Sr Cosmas at Mount Oliver Convent in Dundalk, 2019.

there has been some controversy in the papers about schools, saying that Christmas won't be celebrated. But they're wrong, it will be celebrated but not as I experienced it as a Christian festival. I don't know what they're celebrating. At Christmas, there are beautiful lights, songs, celebrations, presents, excitement, but not a single mention of the birth of Christ. I went into a supermarket and they had a big display of Christmas cards and I couldn't find one with a crib on it. What are they celebrating? When I was growing up, there was a crib in every shop.

> At Christmas there are beautiful lights, songs, celebrations, presents, excitement, but not a single mention of the birth of Christ. I went into a supermarket and they had a big display of Christmas cards and I couldn't find one with a crib on it. What are they celebrating?

'Society now is by and large non-Christian. For me, that is a culture shock. I left a Catholic Ireland. Granted, there was a lot wrong with it and I would be the first to criticise but, at the same time, people believed, and they lived according to Christian principles. Now I find there is a lot of self-centredness. Look at the politicians, they don't seem to care. They've been talking about the same things since I came home, about homelessness, the hospitals, the HSE, trolleys, schools, the lack of teachers – and nothing has changed. Some people believe that the Catholic Church is not necessary, that it's a nuisance, let it die out. People can do that if they want to, but the Church *is* part of our culture. At this point, the Irish in the rest of the world are probably more Irish than we are here.'

'Death Is Part of Life, of Living'

Sr Cosmos has strong views about death. 'Death is part of life, of living. When you think of the universe we are hardly here at all. Our little planet is a tiny speck in the universe and, on that speck, we are smaller specks, hardly there at all. When I think about sin, God couldn't possibly be offended by a little creature like me and what I am doing.'

So does she believe that everyone goes to heaven? 'What do you mean by heaven?' she counters immediately. 'Nobody knows what will happen. I believe there is an afterlife. I believe we will go back to God. We are in God, there's only one life and that is the life of God. We wouldn't exist if God wasn't in us. Creation is one, we are all in the Earth, we are literally made of dust, made of the Earth. We are all one, animals, plants, we are all one. We don't know what is coming next. I would love to be around to see what's going to happen in about two hundred years.

'But people don't want to talk about death, they don't want to think about it. That is my whole thing about teaching. For heaven's sake, children, learn how to think.'

1926: Major Events

World

- UK general strike in support of the coal miners

- Gertrude Ederle becomes the first woman to swim the English Channel

- The future Queen Elizabeth II is born

- Irishwoman Violet Gibson shoots the Italian prime minister, Benito Mussolini, in Rome

- Silent screen star Rudolph Valentino dies aged thirty-one and more than 100,000 people swarm the streets of New York City for his funeral; rioting takes places as fans try to gain entry to the funeral home

- Antoni Gaudí, the architect of Barcelona's La Sagrada Familia, is hit by a tram and dies three days later

- Marilyn Monroe, David Attenborough and Fidel Castro are born

Ireland

- Douglas Hyde officially opens the Irish Free State broadcasting service, 2RN (later RTÉ Radio), in Dublin

- Éamon de Valera resigns as president of Sinn Féin at its árd fheis when one of his proposals is defeated

- A census is held in Ireland, both North and South. The population of the Irish Free State is 2,972,000; the population of Northern Ireland is 1,257,000

- At La Scala Theatre in Dublin a new political party is formed; Fianna Fáil, the Republican Party, is launched by leading republicans including Éamon de Valera and Seán Lemass

- Forty-eight people are burned to death in a cinema fire at Dromcollogher, County

Limerick, when a candle ignites a reel of nitrate film stock

- Éamon de Valera addresses the first Fianna Fáil árd fheis in Dublin

- Gaeltacht areas – regions with a significant percentage of Irish-language speakers – are officially recognised, following the report of the first Coimisiún na Gaeltachta in the Free State

- Seán O'Casey's *The Plough and the Stars* opens at the Abbey Theatre; on 11 February, the performance is marred by ugly scenes as audience members protest at what they claim are historical distortions in the play

- George Bernard Shaw receives the Nobel Prize in Literature but rejects the prize money, asking that it be used to fund the translation of Swedish books to English.

- The Irish Free State football team plays Italy for the first time; Italy win 3–0

- All-Ireland champions: Cork (hurling) and Kerry (football)

A Pulpit for Haughey
Denis O'Callaghan
Born 7 February 1926

A practising violinist, the son of a leading stoker in the British navy and private secretary to Charles J. Haughey, Denis O'Callaghan has led an eventful life. Now ninety-three and still driving, he also has a keen sense of his own family history. 'My parents were Patrick O'Callaghan and Ellen O'Leary. He was from near Ballineen in west Cork, she was from Drimoleague, both of them from small farms. My mother had seven or eight brothers and sisters and, being a small farm, only one would stay and the rest would go, this was in the late 1800s. Several of them went to America and were never heard from again. I'm named after one of them. I think some of them were involved in the bootlegging in the 1930s. They were great people. My mother would have gone to Cork as a young girl.

'My father was the youngest of three. His parents died very early and he was taken over by a family called Duggan. He was reared on the Duggan lands, a bit of an orphan. The parents had been small bakers or shoemakers. He was born in 1883, so around 1900, as a teenager, he would have emigrated to Cork City and got a job there, I know he was working in Haulbowline in the dockyard there. Then, he joined the British navy, which was very common. There was a big recruitment drive by various admirals who lived in Cork, there was a huge tradition of joining the British navy. There was no Irish navy then, no Irish government even. He joined around 1900, and that was his career.

'There was very little said in Cork City afterwards about your navy connections, because of the IRA and the movement in Cork. It wasn't the thing. My father had no political angle on it whatsoever, it was a job for him as a young lad. The stokers were all down shovelling coal. He was described as a "leading stoker".'

During the Second World War, Patrick O'Callaghan served on a ship that was sunk by the Germans. 'The HMS *Warrior*, at the Battle of Jutland, which was a big battle between the British navy and the German navy, which the German navy won. He would say very little about it.

The Brothers

'My mother, then, she went into service and became a cook in a 'Big House' in Cork. She was a great woman, a typical west Cork woman, she was very ambitious for her family. I had four brothers, I am the baby of five. The eldest fella, Patrick, his first job was a telegram boy, then he became a motor mechanic, went to Hull in England, spent most of the war over there working on army vehicles.

'The second fella, Diarmuid, he was an apprentice in a draper's, a place called John Buckley's in Cork. But he was brilliant at artwork, he used to do art and notices for the shop. He came to the notice of Professor Daniel Corkery, who was the local teacher, he encouraged my mother to release him from his job as a draper's assistant, to follow the art, which he did.' Diarmuid got a scholarship and went to the Crawford School of Art in Cork. In 1938, he won the Taylor Scholarship at the Royal Dublin Society with a painting depicting a violent encounter between Irish Travellers and gardaí called *The Struggle*. In 1939, he won the Taylor Prize with *No Peace on Earth*, a painting inspired by the bombing of London that year and the start of the Second World War. He returned to Cork and became a full-time teacher of painting at the Crawford School of Art, from which he retired in 1970. 'I have a number of Diarmuid's paintings, they are brilliant.' Diarmuid's daughter Noël is also a professional artist.

'The third brother was John, he was away to be a Salesian priest at one time, but he got scarlet fever and was encouraged by one of the staff in the hospital to "follow your father into the navy", and so he did that. He was in the navy all through the Second World War, and was on three ships that sank. The last one was the HMS *Curlew*, it was sunk in a fjord in Norway, and he had to swim for shore. He arrived home via the Orkney and the Shetland Islands and Scotland and Northern Ireland and down home, in a big naval jumper which I can still remember was knitted by the Canadian Women's Red Cross for British servicemen. And I was landed with that and I had it for years.

'The fourth one then, Timothy, he was picked for a scholarship. They thought he might go for the priesthood but he didn't go that road, he got a job and he was the first from our little street near Mayfield in Cork, Ashburton Cottages it was called, to get a job in the South Mall, and that was the panacea. He got a job as a clerk, and he worked his way upward, and eventually he was a representative and a kind of a manager in an insurance company, and he married a lady in Galway who was a doctor and they had several children.

'The boys were all born two years apart – 1913, 1915, 1917, 1919, all in the autumn, and it was significant that my father would only be home every couple of years. I was an afterthought, seven years later.'

'The boys were all born two years apart – 1913, 1915, 1917, 1919, all in the autumn, and it was significant that my father would only be home every couple of years.

It was 1943 when Denis left school. 'It was the middle of the war, there was nothing in Ireland for anyone, no jobs in Cork, there would be a couple in the ESB, a couple in the railway, most of the bright boys in the class, loads of them went off to munition factories in England, joined the navy, joined the air force, joined anything to get a job. That year, there were only twenty-four jobs as clerical officers in Ireland. Thousands entered the competition for them and three of us, two pals and myself from the same school, were fortunate to get them – sixth place, eleventh place and seventeenth place.

'I got eleventh place and I went into the civil service. I was assigned to the Registry of Deeds, on Henrietta Street in Dublin. I did not like it. After spending four months there, I got an offer for a job in taxes in Cork, so I jumped on that in about one and a half seconds, and I went back to my mammy and daddy. I was there for a couple of years and then they wanted a crowd of bright young boys in Dublin so I went back to Dublin, and then I got the executive officer and went to the Department of Agriculture, and there I remained for the rest of my career. I was forty-two years there – but I never lost the Cork accent.'

'Yes, Minister'

Denis loved his job and then, one day, he was walking in Stephen's Green. 'I happened to meet the top man in the department, and he said, "I have another job for you. You know we have a new minister, Mr Charles Haughey" – this was in 1965 – "he wants a new private secretary and we have decided on you." So I said, "Well, I have to discuss it with my wife", because it had an implication for my wife and family and all that. And he said, "Oh no, there's no option. You're actually it as of now." So that was it. I was private secretary to Charlie Haughey.'

And, inevitably, I ask the same question he's heard a hundred times before – what was it like to work with Charlie Haughey? 'The first time I met him, he was quite cold, and I was just another tool to be used in the advancement of Charles Haughey, a dogsbody to do everything and anything, which I did successfully, I did the job well. People asked was he nice to work with. No, he wasn't, but every day was exciting because he wanted it exciting. Something was happening every day. He went into Agriculture and knew nothing about it but he had to give the impression – he wanted to be all things to all people, he wanted to be the greatest. If there was going to be a king of Ireland it was going to be him.

'One of the first things he did in 1965 was on the Feast of St Isidore, the patron saint of agriculture. Haughey was advised that it would be a good thing for his advancement to have a special celebration on the feast day, so muggins here was given this job. We had to organise a big mass in the cathedral in Athlone. On the altar, we had two pulpits, one for Charles Haughey and one for Brian Lenihan, and the two of them read the lessons. And, better still, we flew in a friar from Rome to say the mass and the homily and then, afterwards, we had a big shindig in the Hodson Bay Hotel, which at the time was owned by the Lenihan family, and muggins here was down there two nights and organised everything.

On the altar, we had two pulpits, one
for Charles Haughey and one for
Brian Lenihan, and the two of them
read the lessons. And, better still, we
flew in a friar from Rome to
say the mass.

'We had every dog and divil from the world of agriculture, all the top dogs. I knew them all and this was all to advance our friend. He didn't spend any time to get to know agriculture, really. That was a once-off, you could only do that once.'

But despite his misgivings about some of the jobs he was given, Denis says he never had a row with the Boss. 'He regarded me as doing a good job for him, and you don't have a row with a minister. It doesn't help. People say a lot of things against him, but he really had a great sense of humour.

'Appoint Him'

'On one occasion, there was a vacancy that arose for a fisheries inspector, dealing with the Aran Islands and Connemara. It was advertised and the candidate that was selected for the job was an Indian gentleman. When his name came to the office of personnel, they had some reservations about appointing an Indian man as inspector of fisheries in the west of Ireland, so they put this to the minister. "We think there are risks," they said. "Would he get on culturally with the people in the west of Ireland, and how would he cope with the climate in the west of Ireland?"

So Charlie looked at this bit of paper and he

wrote a note on it opposite the "How would he get on culturally with the people in the west of Ireland?" He simply wrote, "Who would?" And under the part about how would he cope with the climate, Charlie wrote, "Get him some warm underwear." And the final note was, "Appoint him." And he was appointed.'

Denis also remembers Haughey's appeal to the opposite sex. 'He had lots of ladies ringing him up. He was very attractive to the ladies. There was one particular lady, I won't say who or what she was, but she was always ringing him.'

'Catholic Girls Did Not Go Out With Protestant Boys'

Denis met his wife, Maureen Hughes from Monaghan, at a dance in the Balalaika Ballroom on Dublin's Dorset Street. 'And would you believe, I have kept the ticket from the dance where I met her. There was a charity dance on there for a lady who was very ill at the time and we all paid half a crown or something to dance. And the lady died on the day of the dance, but the dance went ahead.

'My mother had died in 1949, and I was on the lookout, I suppose, after that. My mother was a

Denis and Maureen's wedding day, 1953.

strong influence in my life, and a wonderful person.
She was very ambitious for her five sons. So after
she died, I felt I needed some female company. I
had lots of girlfriends, but I met this lady at this
dance and I liked her. She was from a Monaghan
background, her father was very tough, and the
idea was that in Monaghan, Catholic girls did not
go out with Protestant boys, because Protestant
boys were only after the one thing. And so she was
very abstemious and upright, always.

Catholic girls did not go out with
Protestant boys, because Protestant
boys were only after the one thing.

'We fell in love, and it was love based on respect and uprightness. That was 1951 we met, we got married in 1953. I can't specifically remember proposing to her, but I do remember we got engaged in the Jesuit church on Gardiner Street. I presented her with a ring which I bought for about thirty-five pounds which was a lot of money at that time. We went there with the intention of getting engaged in front of the Blessed Sacrament.

'Then we went up to see her parents. I remember there were these two men in a bar, and they came towards us and I looked at the two of them and one of them was a lovely jovial man and the other was a grumpy-looking divil, and I said to myself, "Which of them is it?" It was the grumpy old divil. I didn't ask him if I could marry her. It was kind of accepted at that time. She had written to him about it.

And does Denis remember his wedding day? 'I do, well. Central Hotel, Exchequer Street. We had the wedding booked for a place in Rathgar, but they cancelled it in the last week so I had to go round and get a booking elsewhere. There were about twenty people there, very small, down from Monaghan and up from Cork.

'For the honeymoon, we went down to the South Wall and got a boat to the Isle of Man and we were there for ten days or a fortnight. There was a Mrs Cregeen, she was the owner of the hotel, and then – big deal – we came back on a plane. That was Maureen's first flight; I had flown to France and a couple of places as a single fella. We came back here and we had the house in Goatstown for which we paid two thousand pounds.'

The couple had four children. 'A girl, a boy, and two girls, that's the order. The boy is a theologian, a priest in Opus Dei and a professor in a university in Rome, that's Paul. He has written a lot of books. The eldest is Anne, she worked in Trinity College, then she studied economics and psychology and remained in UCD working in administration. Cora went to DIT and studied computers and was with the Teachers Union of Ireland but she spent most of her career in Blanchardstown College of Technology. And then Mary was a clerical officer in the civil service working with Industry and Commerce and then she did a master's in Women's Studies in UCD.'

'Music Was a Huge Thing in My Life'

Denis is an accomplished violinist and, even as we speak, he is preparing to play with the Blow the Dust Orchestra in the National Concert Hall, an orchestra of fifty mature musicians. 'I've a huge interest in music. Music was a huge thing in my life. Instead of going to the university or anything, I took up music. So I am a qualified teacher in both classical and traditional. I didn't do much teaching of the violin but I did some teaching of the mouth organ.'

He is also a well-known Comhaltas Ceoltóirí Éireann musician. 'I've played in fleadhs all over the place, Sligo and Ennis and Cavan. I competed on the violin in the fleadhs, and I was the oldest competitor on the mouth organ in the Ennis fleadh at ninety.'

Denis tells me he is very concerned about the state of Ireland. 'It has totally gone from what we were used to, the Church and all the things we did. The new God is sport. Everything is related to

Denis is a well-known Comhaltas Ceoltóirí musician and still plays the fiddle today.

sport. There was a time when sport happened on a Sunday afternoon. Now there isn't time to go to mass. And television is the other huge influencer. I love my television but there is everything and anything, as bad as you could want, on television.'.

I ask Denis if he is religious. 'Oh definitely. I have a great relationship with the Lord. I talk to Him regularly. I walk around and talk to Him. I have all my own sort of prayers and they are all related to hymns. I talk quite frankly to Him. I'm very well, I have had a great life – I am so grateful. I've a little thing, ACTS – adoration, contrition, thanksgiving and supplication – I deal with those and I get great rewards. I still ask for things and I get nearly everything I ask for. Such stupid things – where did I put this or that, and I always get things. I have a great relationship with Him.

'I don't really relish the idea of being too sick and too unwell and suffering. And I don't want to be offloading my problems on others and being wheelchaired around the place. Death will come; when my time comes I will pop off. I wouldn't like to pop off tonight, like!'

The Best of Linen

Rose Smith

Born 10 February 1926

Rose Smith, aged ninety-three, was born on a farm in Knockmacooney, Summerbank, in Oldcastle, County Meath, the daughter of Patrick Smith and Catherine (Kate) Mahon. Rose attributes her long life to a healthy diet in her youth. 'I was reared on cabbage and bacon. Three times a year, we killed one of our own pigs, we would have the carcase in the box outside, and my mother would go out and cut a bit off and bring it in and hang it up at the fireplace. In the morning, it would be taken down and you'd cut the rashers off it and fry them, and we had plenty of hens and we would always have loads of eggs, and we had a few ducks. The little flock went down to the river beside us every evening, and my father would go down and take them in at night, but one night the fox came and took them all. We had foxes around. We used to have a hunt, the Ballimacud hounds, they hunted once a week.'

But back to the pig-killing. 'There was a man for killing pigs who lived in the area. He would go round everybody and kill their pigs for them. He brought the pig into a shed and hit him with a hammer on the forehead and knocked him out, and then he stabbed him in the side, and the blood came flowing out, and I used to have a can and I would catch the blood. The blood was brought in and left standing, and my mother would put some oaten meal in it. Then the innards were all taken out of the pig and brought in and washed and turned, and we filled them the next day with the blood and we would have black puddings, plenty of them.'

There were eight children in Rose's family, four boys and four girls, and she was the baby, coming after Ned, Maggie, Eoin, Maureen, Tessie, Patsy and Richie. Rose is the only one living now, although most of her siblings reached old age.

They lived a very self-sufficient life on the farm. 'Sure we never went to the shop except for tea and sugar, and my father would buy a big bag of flour. When that would be gone, the bag was taken in, washed, put out on the grass to bleach, and when we had four of them, they would be sewn together and we would have sheets. I was reared on flour bag sheets. It was linen, the best of linen sheets in the end. It was probably common. My aunt had a sewing machine and she would sew them. They were lovely sheets. There was also a trunk with lovely pure linen sheets in it. They'd be used when my uncle came home from America. The bed would be made up and he would get these sheets and, as well, whenever a neighbour died, my mother would take those sheets and lay them out for the neighbour. So those sheets laid out half the country round our place. And they disappeared; they were there until recently, not that long ago.'

I was reared on flour bag sheets. It was linen, the best of linen sheets in the end.

Rose remembers her mother doing everything she could for her brother Richie, who could neither walk nor talk. 'She brought him to Temple

Street Children's Hospital, she brought him all over Dublin, carried him in her arms, went on the train and carried him. He was a long fella with red curls, she brought him round all the places she could where he might get help but there was no cure, he was born that way.'

Wellies in the Ditch

Rose's earliest memory is of an idyllic childhood in Oldcastle where they all went to the local national school. 'I suppose my earliest memory was going to school. We went at four or five and we lived on a big long lane that had rocks and everything, and in the wet weather we would choose that lane, but mostly we went through the fields. We would cross the stile into the field, cross the fields and keep going up to the top of this hill, and other children would come from another part and join us and we would all meet and run down the hill and into the school. We'd come to a ditch near the school, take off our wellingtons and leave them there and put on our shoes for school. We only had a couple of hundred yards to walk to school then.

'We would bring lunch with us, two slices of brown bread and butter, and we would have our dinner when we went home in the evening. The

Rose's father Patrick and dog Spot working on his farm in
Oldcastle, Co Meath.

cabbage and bacon. And for the poor children in
the school, the authorities supplied cocoa. But we
never got cocoa.

Rose loved the freedom of her childhood. 'Going
home from school, I'd often have four or five of
my friends with me and we would play together.

We used to have picnics, they were the trend then and we would have a picnic on the hill. I lived near Lough Crew, the Lough Crew hills. On a Sunday, we used to go up to the heap of stones, there was a long cement stone called The Hag's Chair and there was an indentation for a pipe on the side of it. The caves were open then and you could go in and walk around in the caves. It's all closed up now. Myself and my friends would go. Sometimes, my mother used to take us to a deer park, the deer would be running around.

'And then there was a river that ran at the back of our house, under a bridge, and it expanded like that, and we used to dam the river. We would get a scraw, that's a section of grass cut out in a clump, and then we would get a stone, and we would build it up until it was about the right height, and we would put it across the river and it would stop the flow of water, so we had a swimming pool and we used to spend our days there, very content. We also used to make a tent out of bags in the corner of the field.'

But Rose remembers they were all very obedient children. 'I never got a slap in my life. There was no trouble with any of us with our parents. Never a cross word. I never heard my father say a cross word in his life.'

Christmas was a much quieter affair in Rose's childhood. She remembers helping to make the Christmas pudding but says Santa wasn't around much. Children were usually given something useful such as a pair of shoes. There weren't many toys, although she does remember the occasional doll.

As a teenager, she was aware of the elections taking place. 'I remember the elections and them going around canvassing, two men coming to the house. I loved Dev but, apart from that, we weren't a political family. We weren't too far from the border but we weren't conscious of it, we didn't even go up North until we got a car.'

Nursing Life

Rose went on to secondary school but left in Fifth Year and then stayed at home and looked after her parents and the house. 'I stayed with my parents until my brother, who was living at home, decided to get married. His wife was coming in to the house, and there was no business for me there, so I decided to go off and train as a nurse.'

The idea of becoming a nurse had been there

Rose in her nurse's uniform in London.

ever since her father had fallen while getting out of a car in the yard and had broken his hip. 'As simple as that. My brothers carried him in, carried him upstairs and into the bed, and he never got out of it. He was seven years in bed, and myself and my mother and brothers looked after him. After that, I decided I would train as a nurse. I loved the nursing really.'

Admission was very in-formal in those days. 'I knew the local doctor and his wife, and they introduced me to some doctors in London and their families so they got me into a hospital and I started training as a nurse.' But Rose was twenty-seven when she travelled to Cheam in London to start her training. 'I remember thinking how am I going to get on with these girls who are eighteen and starting? But anyway, we had no problems.' Rose's father was dead at that stage but her mother was very upset about her leaving home. 'Mammy broke her heart crying about me going off to London, "that auld pagan country".'

But Rose had a great life there. 'The people were great to me, all the English, they were very good to me. I nursed all kinds, sirs and lords and ladies.'

> The people were great to me, all the English, they were very good to me. I nursed all kinds, sirs and lords and ladies.

Rose remained in postwar London for four years, completed her training and came back to Ireland. She continued to work as a nurse until she retired at sixty-five.

'There Was Such Saving Long Ago'

People now in their nineties have seen many changes in Irish life. Rose says that many things have improved but that we have lost the old way of living. She cites waste as an example. 'Long ago you would get a coat and when it would begin to wear you would turn it inside out and you would have almost a new coat, so you might have it for years. My brother's collars on his shirts were always turned. There was such saving long ago, it was so different. My father had hard white collars, they had to go to the laundry.'

There have been more definitive changes in recent society that Rose isn't happy with. She says she didn't vote for abortion and, in the case of same-sex marriage, 'I wasn't interested. I didn't bother.' She is reluctant to offer advice to Ireland's young people, however. 'You couldn't give them advice but you can suggest they just do their own thing. And live simply.'

Rose says she is not particularly religious. 'I wouldn't be, but I like to go to mass, I'd be normal. I believe in God, very much so. I believe there is a heaven and a hell. I wouldn't be concerned about dying because we all have to die, it comes to us all. I don't be talking about it. I know it is there, I know it is coming. I would hope to get to heaven but I don't know if I'm good enough.'

Saving Michael Collins

Nora Ryan
Born 27 March 1926

'There was another little baby born two years after me but she died of pneumonia when she was three months old. Her name was Brenda. My dad was mad about Bride, that's what they called her. I don't remember her at all, I was only two. There was nothing to be done for pneumonia then. Her name isn't on the family tombstone but my mother never wanted to talk about it. My mother lost her first little baby too, they call it stillborn today.'

Nora Patricia Walsh was born in Riddlestown, about three miles from Rathkeale, County Limerick. It was a sparsely populated area then. Her parents were Maurice Walsh and Catherine Kenneally and they lived on a small farm. 'My father had to sell a portion of it. He had two brothers and four sisters, and my granny was Mary Ryan – her husband died a young man and left her with six children. Every one of them went on to do well for themselves, there were three teachers. It was a dairy farm mostly, and we had a piggery, rotten yokes of pigs. I didn't help on the farm. I was always mad to get out of it, and said I would never marry a farmer. The man I married, he was able to keep me, and I was able to stay at home. I did accountancy and auditing.'

Nora had two surviving sisters, Ita and Theresa. 'So my father had plenty of daughters. He was mad about us all. He was lovely. Times were hard, especially trying to pay for college, but an uncle of mine helped out because my father had given him money when he was setting up his business.' She describes her family as 'average'; they weren't hungry, they had enough but they were put to the pin of their collar to keep things going.

Self-Reliance

As with all family farms of the time, the Walshes were self-reliant when it came to food production. 'They killed their own pig and cured it. When they killed the pig, the pig could be heard for miles around. Screeching. My mother was the cook, she made puddings and sausages out of it. And you know the pork steak that's so much money now? You'd be sent after school, and every cottage along the road would be given a bit. To think what we were giving away!

'And then my mother would be trying to fool us and give us the liver because she had all the pork steak gone. And we would say, "That's liver." And she would say, "Oh you know too much." She would give you what she had. There was a rocking cot that she would get thousands for now, and it was one of the richer people of the family, one of the Cahills, that gave it to her, a beautiful rocking cot, and she had a rocking chair, and she gave them away.'

Saving Michael Collins

Nora tells me her father was a Michael Collins man. 'Like every young person around for miles. Jeekers, they would die for Michael Collins. They called themselves Collins' men, they hated the sight of de Valera. Sean Finn was their commander. He is buried in Rathkeale.' Sean Finn was one of the major figures of the period. He was killed in action on 30 March 1921 near Foynes in County Limerick after he and his men were attacked by three lorry loads of Black and Tans.

Nora has her father's version of events. 'Sean Finn was on a bridge on the River Dee, it's a tributary, eventually goes into the Shannon, it's only a mile from us at home. There were about a hundred of Finn's men there, they came from all over, they were going to put a bomb under the bridge. Sean Finn, he was the ringleader, and he nearly had it done, and the whole lot of them escaped through the fields but poor Sean Finn stood his ground to finish putting it in, and they riddled him. He was killed. I think everyone in Ireland knew about it. The bomb didn't go off because he didn't finish it.'

The Black and Tans then went to Mrs Finn's house. 'Everyone knew her, because Sean Finn was the top man, he was the boss, the leader of the crowd. And the Tans went to her door, and said, "We have your son in the lorry." And she was delighted, the way he said it she thought they just had him captured. And then they said "his body". It was so cruel. It made the boys go mad altogether, isn't it a wonder they weren't all killed. The day of his funeral, the graveyard was full. Everyone risked their lives to be there, they were all being watched by the Tans and if you looked crooked at them, there would be a massacre.'

Nora's family also played a major part in providing a safe house for Michael Collins. 'My father told me, he kept Michael Collins. Collins was on the run and he kept him safe. He hid in an attic in our house, you would never think there was a bedroom there, it was well concealed but it was a grand bedroom. They put up a little stairs, kind of hidden in a press and you'd open the press and there would be pots and frying pans and you would never think there would be somebody upstairs.

Michael Collins was on the run and he kept him safe. He hid in an attic in our house, you would never think there was a bedroom there, it was well concealed but it was a grand bedroom. They put up a little stairs, kind of hidden in a press and you'd open the press and there would be pots and frying pans and you would never think there would be somebody upstairs.

'He had a bed there, whenever he would come. There was a window, a good big window, like a Georgian window and he would slip down in the morning, at three or four o'clock, into the flowerbed and off through the fields. The Tans wouldn't be up till six or seven. That was in Heafy Lodge in Riddlestown, where I grew up. My father told Collins there was a bed there for him any time. And, sure, why wouldn't he? It was tough on my mother, though, we would have been very young.

'The war years were tough too. My mother had the sergeant in with her and she said, "God, all our rations are gone." And he said, "I'll get rations for you. They'll be a bit dearer." And she said, "Oh what harm about that." And he told us that he'd deal with Hitler, if necessary. So there was this fella in Rathkeale, he had a dance band and he was an undertaker as well so he had a hearse. He went up North with an empty coffin, the same as if he was going to bury someone, and he came down with it filled with cigarettes, sugar, the lot.'

From Sally Rods to a New Secondary School

Nora describes her primary school as very primitive. 'I remember the sally rods. The Sixth

Class would be sent out for the sally rods to hit the boys and girls. There were only two teachers, two rooms – a big room and a small little room, where you had infants, senior infants, first and second, and a teacher in there with them. But they were only little. But then you had third, fourth, fifth and sixth in the other – no wonder she had to have the sally rod.'

There was no secondary school in the area at the time but a former seminarian at Maynooth started one up just before Nora finished primary school. 'It was the best thing that ever happened. He was tough but he had brains. His name was Jack O'Connor, from Kerry. I will remember him to my dying day. He would turn around in class and say, "You didn't pay your fees." We had to pay fees three times a year in secondary.' The students in the new school studied Irish, English, Latin and French. 'It's a pity they didn't do German, because of Brussels and everything. I loved Latin, though.' Nora says nine students continued through to doing their Leaving Certificate. After school, she went on to study accountancy.

There were many Travellers living in Rathkeale when Nora was growing up and they got on well with the settled community. 'They were grand. We always brought them in and gave them a cup of tea. There was one old man, Jim Kavanagh, people used to be afraid but we were mad about him. He had an auld bag on his back and went everywhere.'

'God, There's Something about Him'

When she finished her accountancy course, Nora got a job straightaway. 'They saw my marks – the Irish Agricultural Wholesale Society (IAWS). I still have the two letters they sent me wishing me luck on my wedding. They said they were sorry about the paper. It was during the war years and the paper was brown, the stationery was rotten stuff.'

Her new husband was definitely *not* a farmer. 'I said I would never marry a farmer and I got all my wishes. I met him at a teachers' dress dance, I only went along to make up the numbers.' In a complicated story, Nora says she was giving a lift home to a friend who was a teacher and another teacher insisted that Nora would go to the dance. That girl, another Nora, turned out to be Michael's sister, the man *our* Nora would eventually marry.

'I said I would go for the fun of it and I went but I didn't go with anyone. I went as a schemer. I was going out with someone else at the time anyway. I would have married him.' The dance was in

Cappamore. 'I forget what I was wearing exactly, I had a lovely dress all right, I think it was navy with a little flick. And I danced all night, I danced with several lads. I spotted Michael standing at the door, but I didn't know he was Nora Ryan's brother. So he asked me to dance, he didn't mean anything to me, but he was back again a couple of dances later, and I said to myself, *God, there's something about him. You could trust him.* And bejaysus, he won in the end. Michael was a bee inspector and he went around checking the hives.'

Nora tells the story of her close friend, Josie. 'She was a friend of mine from the dancing days. I was pure mad about her, she was lovely. She was engaged to be married, but didn't she get breast cancer. I was so sorry for her. It was as if my sister had it. She had her fiancé, Pat O'Brien was his name and he had a big farm. Pat stood by her, with the chemo and everything; we all danced together, laughed together. But thankfully she survived and had a little child after a good few years. Isn't that marvellous? We were friends since we were sixteen and went to college together.'

Nora and Michael started going out. 'When we were courting, he would come into Limerick

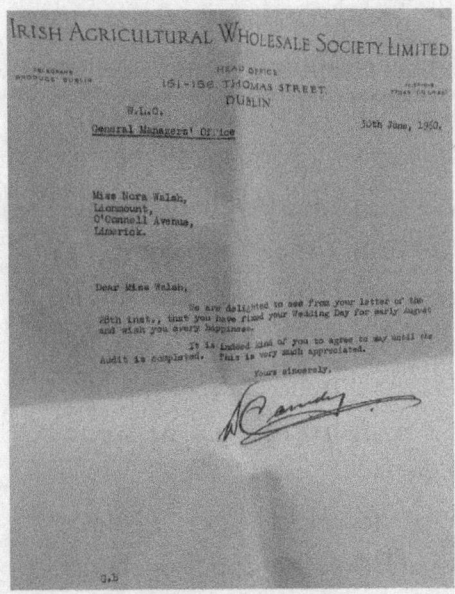

A letter of appreciation to Nora
from IAWS.

where I was working and take me out to a meal.' Then he proposed. 'Well, I knew damn well it was coming, it was no surprise to me. I felt like he wasn't trusting me, he wanted the wedding to be sooner.' But her company wanted her to do an audit before she left work. 'So I put off the wedding till August. We had a lovely wedding, in Ardhu House in Limerick. It was a beautiful place for photographs. I had a champagne-coloured dress, the new dresses were in at the time, they were shorter and I had a champagne headdress. Beautiful. I didn't bother with the white.'

Head office sent Nora a letter thanking her for staying for the audit, and from the staff there was a wallet of notes. 'It was lovely. And a cheque for a hundred smackers. I was pure delighted. My wages were 600 pounds a year. I bought a car, a four-door Morris Minor, taxed it and insured it, and I had change out of 500 old pounds. When I told our lads today they laughed and said you wouldn't get the tyres for that now.'

They went on honeymoon up the west. 'There was no one going foreign at that time. And then we ended up south, in Tramore. We had a grand fortnight.'

Illness – and an Odd Discovery

But Nora became ill, she was diagnosed with cancer while still only in her twenties. This entailed a hysterectomy, and Nora was amazed by a very odd discovery. 'If you were a Catholic, you had to have your husband's permission at the time to get your womb removed! Michael was asked by the doctor and he said, "It's Nora I want." But getting cancer so young, it was an awful shock. I thought I would have a big family. But sure I did, I adopted three children: Michael Gerard and Matthew Joseph, after my father-in-law, and I always said if I had a little girl I would call her Mary, and I did.'

Nora's eldest sister, Ita, became a nun and taught French and English, and it was through Ita's order that Nora's children were adopted.

Nora's other sister, Theresa, thought school would never end. 'She wouldn't go to any secondary school. She was mad into greyhounds and she would train them and have her night out in Limerick. She got married but buried her husband very young, and was left with two small children. He got acute leukaemia. He was given six months to live and was dead and buried in the six months.'

As regards present-day Ireland, Nora is very concerned about emigration. 'Mary, my daughter, is a nurse, and she said she would take off her hat to any young nurse, they have to go off abroad and they get twice what they get here and they will never fix that.'

Religion is very important to Nora. 'Only for my religion, I wouldn't be here. I am a firm believer. The thorns with the roses. Those who don't practise, I leave it to themselves. I preach no sermons.'

Nora always exercises her franchise, voting no in the abortion referendum and yes to same-sex marriage. 'The way I look at it, I think the priests are wrong, the same God made all of us, some just a little different.'

The Clock Is Ticking

'My husband died in 2005; he is waiting for me for fourteen years. Sure I'm ninety-three and the clock is ticking.' Regarding death, she says she hopes she is ready. 'And I hope He will make it as light as He can for me. I don't be thinking about it. I believe in an afterlife, not like here. Sure we must only be a little dot in the universe.

'I am hoping to meet up with all the people I've loved. But I don't believe we will be left as we are now and that we will know each other and say, "Hello, hello!" But sure how will we know? I don't understand it so I wouldn't give you an opinion. Who knows what's going to happen?'

What advice would Nora give to young people today? 'To love one another, forgive one another. And to

Nora Ryan, 2019.

give help when needed, and give a shoulder to cry on. We are doing an inter-generational choir with the local school and the song is 'Always Be Humble and Kind'. That's lovely. People hold grudges and that drives me mad. And it's over nothing. I hate to see people who can't have a cup of tea together.'

Gathering the Hay

Sabina Tierney
Born 17 July 1926

Sabina Tierney was born in Curragh, near Cloonfad in County Galway. Her family lived in a thatched cottage that had the traditional 'hag' or bed in the kitchen. She was the daughter of Bridget and Thomas Moran, who had seven children; Sabina's six siblings have all passed away. 'I was the baby of the family, two of my sisters went to England and three of them went to America but I stayed at home.' In fact, the furthest Sabina has travelled in her long life was to south Kerry where she had relatives.

Sabina can remember her parents' political allegiance. 'My people were Fine Gael. All the village was. They didn't believe in de Valera, they didn't like him. He put a tariff on cattle. And next thing, you were selling the finest cattle for three or four pounds, where you would get a lot more before that.'

Growing up, she worked on the family farm, which produced cattle, horses and potatoes. 'I went out in the harvest and gathered the hay and sowed the potatoes.'

There was no transport to the local school so Sabina and her brother and sisters had to walk two miles each way. When she left school at fifteen, she helped at home with housework and again on the farm. She remembers the difficulties of the war years. 'Everything was rationed, tea and sugar and flour. There was only brown flour, some could make cakes out of it. My mother used to sift it with the white flour. It was like pig food but people had to make do with it.'

> Everything was rationed, tea and sugar and flour. There was only brown flour, some could make cakes out of it. My mother used to sift it with the white flour. It was like pig food but people had to make do with it.

Ballroom of Romance

Then she met the love of her life, Thomas Paul Tierney, at a dance in Cloonfad. 'I knew him for years, so we started dating, going to the dance hall.' But they didn't get around to marrying until six years later – in Ballinalough in 1957 – and Sabina remembers that she wore a blue coat and hat. Her new mother-in-law organised the wedding breakfast in her house. But there was no honeymoon; her new husband was a busy farmer and looking after the farm was their priority. 'It was just back to work as usual the next day. A lot of people did that then, or they might just go away for a day or two.'

> But there was no honeymoon;
> her new husband was a busy farmer
> and looking after the farm
> was their priority.

The couple had two children, Pádraig and Irene, but she says life as a young woman was tough. 'It wasn't rosy but people made do as best they could.

Sabina with her two children,
Pádraig and baby Irene, and their
cousin, Mary Moran, c.1966.

I had my son in Roscommon and my daughter in Tuam. You would stay in hospital much longer then. Tuam was a lovely place, it was a nursing home and they would keep you there, they wouldn't let you out. It was like heaven. Roscommon wasn't that good.'

Sabina is not impressed with much of today's Ireland. 'The young people, how they dress and how they act, it's not like it was one time. I think we were happier then. Nowadays, it's nothing but who will have the biggest wedding, who will have the fanciest headstone in the cemetery, and that's the way Ireland has gone now.'

She says she believes in God and in an afterlife. 'But no one ever comes back to tell the story. So what you don't see is hard to believe. I believe in a heaven. I'll have to go to know what it's like, I would say it is beautiful.'

And her advice to young people? 'They mightn't have any heed for me, but I would tell them to go to mass and say their prayers and believe in God, and not to get into any sinful activities. The world has gone very wicked.'

Sabina at Central Park Nursing Home in Ballinasloe, 2019.

1927: Major Events

World

- Charles Lindbergh flies the *Spirit of St Louis* across the Atlantic non-stop, landing in Paris

- An earthquake in Xining, China, kills 200,000 people

- The first transatlantic telephone call is made, between New York City and London

- Roger Moore, Gina Lollobrigida and the future Pope Benedict XVI are born

Ireland

- The general election leads to a hung Dáil, with Fianna Fáil entering the chamber for the first time and removing Cumann na nGaedheal's majority

- In a radio broadcast, the leader of Fianna Fáil, Éamon de Valera, says that the results of the general election prove that the people of Ireland want to get rid of the Oath of Allegiance

- A morning solar eclipse takes place across Ireland

- Kevin O'Higgins, Vice-President of the Executive Council and Minister for Justice, is assassinated by the anti-Treaty Irish Republican Army in Dublin

- Constance Markievicz (née Gore-Booth) dies aged fifty-nine; she was an officer in the Irish Citizen Army, taking part in the Easter Rising and the first woman elected to the British House of Commons, though she did not take her seat; she was also the first female Irish cabinet minister

- Ireland's first automatic telephone exchange is opened in Dublin

- Ernest Bewley opens his Grafton Street café

- The Electricity Supply Board (ESB) is established as an offshoot of the Shannon Scheme

- All-Ireland champions: Dublin (hurling) and Kildare (football)

The Birth of a New Ireland

Eithne Lee
Born 4 June 1927
Maree O'Leary
Born 8 June 1927

Their parents went to school together, they were born just four days apart and they finish one another's sentences. Maree O'Leary and Eithne Lee live in the Dublin suburb of Raheny, and they have so many similar interests, and such a shared past, that they decided to be interviewed together.

Maree's parents were Michael O'Colmaín and May Coll, from Donegal. The couple had three children – Donal, Maree and Eoin. May was the principal of Clonsilla National School, a huge three-storey building. 'The pathway went down from the school and that was our house.' The school was built when the royal canal was being dug out. 'It was a big mound of land and the school was built on that. They were very lucky to get this land. We used to call it the banks. On the pathway on

the way to the school,
there were fully grown
trees either side, and we
used to play running
from one to the other.'

But did she get
special treatment being
the teacher's daughter?
'I kept quiet, just in
case,' she says.

Her earliest memory
is when she was
about three. 'We had
a housekeeper and
we were standing at
a bus terminus and
she was chatting up

Maree (left) and brother
Donal, 1927.

the bus conductor. She said, "You can have her."
Meaning me. He must have said I was a nice child
or something. I was terrified he was going to take
me away, that's why I remember it so well.'

She also remembers another, more pleasant,
incident when she was five. 'At the school, there
was a high steppy place where you could stand
and the postman arrived and he had a parcel for

me. When I opened it there were two pairs of ankle socks, beautiful colours.'

She still recalls being very bad at spelling and bringing sandwiches for lunch. 'At lunch hour, we all went out and played football and hopscotch with an old polish tin.'

Eithne says she played skipping, tag and blindman's bluff. 'There was a lot of poverty then.'

'The boys had big hob-nailed boots,' Maree adds.

'And some had no boots at all.' Eithne again. 'There were cottages down the road and they were very poor, cottages where the father, the breadwinner, had gone to England to work. It was the children who suffered.'

The Construction of Dublin Airport

Eithne grew up where Dublin airport is now. 'There was an aerodrome that bordered our farm, the British troops used it in the First World War. And, in 1937 or 1938, it was taken over by the Irish state. There was a compulsory acquisition order on my father's farm. They paid three thousand pounds between the six farms around the airport, ours was fifty acres, a mixed farm, cattle and arable and vegetables of every description. They had carts going to the market, orange carts, and they had pyramids of green cabbage. And I used to see them going off to market early in the morning, into the Dublin market. I wrote a bit of poetry about it, 'Farewell to the Fingal Road'.

The building of the airport, which started in 1936, was the major event in Eithne's childhood and, proving the fact that Ireland really is a very small place, another interviewee for this book, Tom Stack who now lives in County Clare, later worked as an engineer on the construction of one of the runways. 'I was about ten when the building started. My father had had a stroke the previous year and was invalided. My mother had to take over. There was barely enough money from the sale of the house to buy another one. My mother was a very efficient woman and she would go on her bike all over North County Dublin looking for somewhere to buy. She was a great character. Finally, she found a piece of land in the Baskin, she found this field, two and a half acres, and she got a small bungalow built on it. She even supervised the building work. In the meantime, we had to stay with neighbours, they demolished our house and

Eithne (right) and her sister
Meabh.

we had to move. They were lovely people. We stayed with them for a whole winter.' Eithne's father died when he was just fifty-eight.

But the family enjoyed watching the airport being built on their land. 'My mother was in her element because she was from Ballybough and all her people are buried there, and she was meeting people she knew coming to work on their bikes to the airport. She loved entertaining, there were always people in our kitchen, having tea on the way home from work.'

Eithne had just one sister, Meabh, and her earliest memories revolve around her medical treatment. 'It was for something between her eyes and she was operated on when she was very young. I remember her coming home from the hospital. This doctor was before his time, Dr Carville. He lived down in Edenmore House and when we'd be passing in the pony and trap, my mother would say, "That's where Dr Carville lives." But Meabh was always kind of pampered then and I was left to plough my own furrow. She was a year and a half younger than me. I remember them bringing her home after she was born and it was the first time I saw blue rubber knickers. They had no plastic nappies. For nappies you would cut up old sheets or pillowslips or whatever. A lot of work.'

Republican Allegiances

Both women were very conscious of the birth of a new Ireland and the turmoil involved for many families. Both of Eithne's parents were with the Fingal Brigade coming up to the Rising. 'They were very republican. I was very proud of my father, he was very patriotic. He was a hero in my eyes. He was interned in Frongoch in Wales after the Rising. He was the only one in his family involved. We were very aware that my father and all his friends had fought for the new state. It was strange how it happened, really.

'My father would speak in Irish to his friend Tomás. He had gone to Irish classes in St Margaret's.

There would be a knock on the door and if we heard "*Conas atá tú?*" it was Tomás Colmaín.'

Eithne's house was also used to shelter rebels on the run. 'We didn't look on it like that … but I suppose we *were* a safe house when things were really hot.'

'My uncle went on hunger strike,' says Maree. 'My mother and father had to go and learn Irish. Bean de Valera, who later married Éamon de Valera, taught my father.'

> My mother and father had to go and
> learn Irish. Bean de Valera, who later
> married Éamon de Valera, taught
> my father.

'Little Miss Flanagan they called her,' Eithne adds. 'People loved her, and always wanted to carry her books. And then along came the long yellow Spaniard.'

'And she was no more interested in anyone once he came along,' says Maree.

'He used to come to her *rang Gaeilge*,' says Eithne. 'It was a voluntary Irish class.'

Then Maree remembers a friend who had a brother in the British army and another in the IRA. One time, when the brother from the British army was home on holiday in Swords, the Black and Tans raided the house. But when they saw the army hat on the table they said, 'Oh bloody hell, we've got the wrong place.'

'And they were going to have a new country all their own,' says Maree. 'Their own language, their own money ... I miss the money. With the little pigs and the horses.'

'And they were going to have a new country all their own,' says Maree. 'Their own language, their own money ... I miss the money. With the little pigs and the horses.'

There are the comforting memories too for the ladies, including the food they ate as children. 'Once a week, we had rabbit,' says Maree. 'Nobody really eats rabbit anymore.'

'I didn't eat rabbit until after I was married,'

Eithne tells me. 'My husband Brendan was very fond of rabbit and he had a friend that used to bring him some. People earned a living by selling rabbits, there were lots of rabbits about.'

'And we would eat mutton,' says Maree.

'And bacon,' Eithne adds.

'The only sweets we had then were NKMs and you could get ten for a penny,' Maree says. 'I don't know what NKM stood for, it was like toffee with a little bit of peppermint in it. It was lovely.'

'We had Honeybees for ten a penny. And Nancy balls or aniseed balls,' Eithne recalls.

'And Peggy's leg ... nice! And liquorice pipes.' Maree is getting hungry at the thought.

'We would have had no money, no pocket money,' says Eithne. 'But we had homemade cakes, my mother had a griddle and she used to make griddle cake. It didn't rise very much.'

You weren't allowed in because you were a child and you would sit on the steps and they would bring you out lemonade. That was lovely.

'I loved it when we were out somewhere, driving somewhere,' Maree recalls, 'and the adults went in for a pint. You weren't allowed in because you were a child and you would sit on the steps and they would bring you out lemonade. That was lovely.'

Music and Painting

There are musical memories too. 'When I was very small,' says Eithne, 'my father played the fiddle, and he used to have these sessions in the kitchen around the fire. There was a friend of his, Jimmy Bennett, played the fiddle as well. Traditional musicians. My uncle Pat played the squeezebox, and there would be other neighbours in. My parents were very disappointed I couldn't sing, I was like a crow. They sent both myself and Maeve to piano lessons but I had no luck.'

'I played the cello and the piano,' Maree says. 'I went in for the Father Matthew Feis.'

Both women are accomplished painters. Eithne started when she was very young. 'I was always interested. It was in my father's family, there were a few nuns who were very handy. I painted in a very old copybook. I gave up the painting recently, my eyes.'

'I wanted to be an artist,' says Maree. 'I didn't do it in school, and then, later on, when I'd had a number of children, I went back to classes. And then they asked me would I *give* a class to senior citizens.'

But she credits her mother for her interest in drawing. 'I remember my first copybook which I got when I was three or four. My mother wrote my name on it and I was annoyed because I wanted to write my own name myself. So she scribbled my name out and I was even more annoyed then because she had scribbled it out. So she saw I was annoyed, and she turned each scribble into a little bird. She put heads on them and I was amazed. And from then I was scribbling on my copybooks.'

Education and Training

Maree was sent to Loreto College. 'But I was too young really. They had just started the Irish section of it, I was only nine and a half when I went. For the first six months, I was a day pupil, and then the war started in 1939 – I was twelve when the war broke out.'

She decided to go to UCD to study medicine. 'But coming from a girls' school, I hadn't done physics, I hadn't done chemistry, it was all a new language to me. There were three hundred in the class and I knew I hadn't a hope. So I met a girl who was doing physiotherapy, she was from Dunboyne, and she was telling me about it and I thought, *Now that's what I'd like*. So I switched. In those days, the School of Physiotherapy was on Hume Street, and I went there for about a year and then I went over to England and went to West Middlesex Hospital to finish my studies.'

Maree's first job in Ireland was part-time between St Vincent's Hospital and Cherry Orchard. I had a scooter, there was no bus up to Cherry Orchard in the beginning. Then I moved to the new Fever Hospital in Cork Street. It was very interesting, the wards were one big long room with one big table. Some of the children were there for a year because they got scarlet fever and they would be sitting all along the table doing scribbling and drawing.' She remembers her wages were three pounds, twelve shillings and six pence per week.

Eithne went to secondary school with the Sisters of Charity in King's Inns Street. 'It was a very popular school back then, it was a state school but it was always looked upon as a very good school.' But there was no question of going to university. 'In Swords we had a borough, and there were councillors, but that disbanded in 1891 and the money was to be used for the education of the children in Swords. But the money was only spent on the Protestant children. Two uncles of my father's from Fosterstown called a meeting in Swords and they wanted the Catholic kids to be included. And they won.

'There was a competition held with a first prize of twenty pounds, the second was fifteen pounds and the third was twelve pounds. But I only got 25 per cent for singing 'Oró Sé Do Bheatha 'Bhaile' and I must have made a show of myself. But, anyway, they wouldn't give me the prize because we were half a mile outside the parish. And the parish priest came up to my mother and apologised profusely, he did his level best to get it for me. It was a lot of money back then and remember my mother was a widow at that stage.'

When she left school, Eithne got into the civil service. 'First the telephone exchange and then the GPO. The first time I was left on my own I was asked to get Ballaghaderreen 2, and I had never heard of it. The girl beside me was more senior and I said to her, "Where in the name of God is Ballaghaderreen?"'

Despite working in the city, Eithne regrets that she never climbed Nelson's Pillar. But Maree did. 'During the war. And I was amazed. Clerys was across the road and on top of Clerys there were piles and piles of stuff, clothes and all. Storage I suppose. It cost threepence to go up the Pillar.'

Clerys was across the road and on
top of Clerys there were piles and
piles of stuff, clothes and all. Storage
I suppose. It cost threepence to go
up the Pillar.

The Men in Their Lives

Eithne got married when she was twenty-one. 'No wonder you had ten children!' Maree laughs.

'I met my husband, Brendan, at home,' Eithne tells me. 'In the bungalow, the new bungalow that my mother had built, my father was dead at this stage. I got to know this girl, Josie Nolan, she was doing a line with a fella called Charlie Lee, from Griffith Avenue. It was the summer of 1946, and Charlie and Josie used to come out to me, cycle out to me in the Baskin. But one day, instead of Charlie

Eithne and Brendan's wedding,
3 January 1949.

coming with Josie, it was his brother, Brendan. And that was it.

'My mother was crazy about him. He was a mathematician but when he found these two orphaned girls, myself and my sister, all he wanted to do was farm.' So Eithne met the love of her life and that was that? But she corrects me. 'He fell in love with me, I didn't fall in love with him.'

Brendan took over the farm and one summer planted a half acre of celery. 'Celery needs an awful lot of water, and he spent that summer up and down to the quarry bringing up the water. My mother had opened a shop for sundries, she was the kind to never let the grass grow under her feet.' Eithne's mother died the same year, and just before Eithne and Brendan were married. 'Nowadays, it would be elementary enough, but her spleen burst. They removed the spleen but the poison had gone through her at that stage.'

The couple were married in the church in Swords and the wedding breakfast was held in the Metropole on O'Connell Street. 'There were only thirty-seven people. It was in January and I wore what they called a costume, a powder-blue jacket and dress. And we were married early in the morning, probably eight o'clock. The honeymoon was in Cork in the Windsor Hotel.' Then it was back to the Baskin, 'because Brendan had the cattle'.

But Eithne didn't know then that she had signed up for a lifetime of GAA duties. Brendan became secretary of the GAA in Raheny, the club is now named after him for his tremendous work on behalf of the organisation. But Eithne got the job of washing the jerseys. 'I had to wash the jerseys for the entire team and then he was put in charge of the Dublin minors and I only had a very elementary type of washing machine. It had a mangle on it and one Sunday night

Maree with her father on her
wedding day, 1958.

I was washing the jerseys and my whole arm went in. I screamed. They were all watching television, then someone ran and pulled out the plug. I survived but it was very sore for a while.'

Maree met her husband, John Joe O'Leary, when she was working as a physiotherapist in Cherry Orchard Hospital. 'There was an epidemic of polio at that time so there were physiotherapists needed. He came to Cherry Orchard, he was a doctor, John Joe O'Leary from Cork, near Mallow. He was there to study all sorts of diseases. Cherry Orchard was made up of groups of bungalows so that the disease wouldn't spread. So to get to the main building, I would have to walk up. John had a little Volkswagen at the time and I was walking up one day and he stopped and asked me could he give me a lift. Three years later, we were married.' The couple had six children, four boys and two girls.

Children and Grandchildren

This talk of babies brings us to the topic of childbirth. 'You didn't dwell on it. There was no fuss,' says Maree.

'It was so primitive,' Eithne adds. 'I remember for my first child Tony's birth in 1950, I had to pull on a sheet. There were two nurses and I had to pull on a sheet. I don't remember any painkillers. The second fella came so quickly he was born at home. A neighbour delivered him, she was as good as any nurse. It was about six in the morning and Brendan ran up for her.'

'She probably had done that for a lot of people,' says Maree.

'Having ten children was normal enough in those days,' Eithne tells me. 'I had five boys and five girls.'

'Having ten children was normal enough in those days,' Eithne tells me. 'I had five boys and five girls.'

'As de Valera would say, God bless you,' Maree laughs.

'We had the farm and the shop and we didn't know what a night's sleep was,' says Eithne. 'The eldest fella was asthmatic and every night it was "Mammy, Mammy!" Never "Daddy"! I'd sometimes have to put his head out the window to get him air. It was tough enough going. But towards the end, the older ones were grown up and they could help with the younger ones. In the beginning, there was only a year or so between each of them but the last few there were three and four years between them. Now I have twenty-six grandchildren and the ninth great-grandchild is on the way.'

Maree has seven grandchildren.

'Very often the same person that delivered babies laid out dead people too,' says Maree. 'The only one I remember dying was a little girl, about twelve, maybe younger. She was a twin, and the brother was in hospital, and he was coming home this day and she was terribly excited and she ran across the road and she was run over. That is the only death I remember.'

'I remember a teacher we had,' says Eithne, 'Mrs

Birmingham. She was from Donegal, and we went to her funeral, that was traumatic. We loved her. She died after the birth of her twins but her twins lived. And in Swords, if there was ever a death, we all trooped in to say a prayer. I remember a little child had died and we all had to go in and see the little baby laid out.'

Eithne's husband Brendan died in 2000 and her only sister died in the same month. Maree's husband John died two years later. 'He got cancer of the throat when he was eighty-two.'

'It's Really Noisy Now'

So what do the two friends think of the country they live in now?

'It was calmer,' says Maree. 'It's really noisy now. If you go into a café, they are laughing and shouting and screaming, and you're trying to talk nice and quietly.'

'That's because our ears are bad,' Eithne explains. 'Our hearing aids. I've had them for years.'

They have hope in the future of the country.

'I would like to see homes for people,' Marie says.

'People are different these days,' says Eithne, 'they expect more.'

'I would quite like Northern Ireland to become part of the Republic,' Maree says. 'People say, it couldn't happen, but then look at the Berlin Wall. It came down. Things start gradually in this life, then bang and they're there.'

'Religion is different now too,' adds Eithne. 'When we were growing up we knew our limitations and the ten commandments and the priest. But now we have nothing to lean on. Young people today have nothing to lean on, no barrier.'

'Well, they did tell us a load of rubbish and lies over the years,' says Maree, 'and now we're quietly unravelling it all.'

'Last Sunday, they spoke about Adam and Eve, *God taking the bone from Adam to make Eve*,' Eithne says.

'That's all right for children,' Maree replies, 'but when you grow up you don't accept it.'

'I'm beginning to think that Luther was born in the wrong time,' says Eithne.

'And it took them three hundred years to tell us that he shouldn't have been excommunicated,' Maree says. 'That's the pace they go at.'

'He was trying to clean up the Church,' says Eithne.

'And poor Pope Francis is over there trying to do the same,' adds Maree. 'I go to mass and I give out and I give out. I go to St Brigid's. There used to be a man in Raheny – we used to go to mass in Raheny when John was alive – and he used to answer the priest. The priest would say, "Do this in memory of me", and he'd say, "Not you, you're an imposter!"'

Valerie Cox

Farewell to Fair Fingal
(on first travelling on the new M50)
Eithne Lee

Farewell, farewell to fair Fingal,
Its pastures green and laneways small,
Its woodlands deep and fields of corn
Farewell to cuckoo, lark and thrush
To birch and oak and hawthornbush.

The slow farm-horse to market bound,
The red farm-cart with produce found
In gardens, farmland all around
In convoy made a happy sound.

Where is Tubberbunny now and Cuckoo Lane
And Collinstown and Pickardstown?
And Forest Great and Little?
And the road that led to that grand old house
Where Peadar played the fiddle.

Alas! today there's concrete grey of great
highway
Where traffic roars and pollution soars
And green fields gone forever
Oh why the speed and why the need
Of all this frantic hurry
When Fingal was a quieter place
We got there without worry.

Overcoming Religious Division
Pauline Hilliard
Born 29 June 1927

Pauline begins by telling me the story of how her mother and father met. 'She was such a marvellous person. She was one in about ten million. Her name was Elizabeth Rowntree, she was Elizabeth Ryan before she married. She was from a village five miles from Castlerea where we lived, in Roscommon. She was a farmer's daughter, but my dad was an Armagh man, and he came to Castlerea, after he had had a falling out with his family. He was married and had four children, two boys and two girls but, unfortunately, his wife had died. My mum married him then and took over those four children. They weren't going to any homes, they were going to be brought up with them. So she had those four and she reared eight of her own after that. Twelve children. She was a marvellous woman.'

And when times were tough, Elizabeth Rowntree shared with everybody. 'You never heard her complain. She would make that loaf stretch ... maybe there might be a tomato in the cupboard, she would always get the bit for whoever came in. A kind woman. The tinkers used to come around, and my mum's back door opened onto the street. They were always good; say you had a leaking saucepan, the saucepan wasn't flung out because it was leaking, it was held until the tinkers came and fixed it.'

The tinkers used to come around, and
my mum's back door opened onto
the street. They were always good;
say you had a leaking saucepan, the
saucepan wasn't flung out because
it was leaking, it was held until the
tinkers came and fixed it.

Pauline was the sixth of the eight children of her father's second marriage. 'There was the eldest, Tommy, then Joe, then Pearse, the three boys came first. Then my eldest sister, Loreto, but she was christened Loreto Markievicz after the countess. Then there was Patricia. Then there was *mise*, myself. Then Éamonn, and the youngest, Philomena. The other four children, as soon as they came to be in their teens, two of them went back to the North, because all Dad's family were in the North, but they didn't go to his actual home, they went to friends.

Religious Division

'There was an awful split. Dad, Lord have mercy on him, was Protestant. Mum was Catholic. And Dad had to turn to marry Mum, which really caused the trouble in the family. They didn't like that at all. But down the years, they made it up and, in fact, they even gave the Catholic Church a piece of their land in Armagh, to build a little church. We never got to meet my dad's parents, they weren't talking at that stage. They were gone before we got in close contact with his brothers.'

Pauline's Armagh family were in the furniture business so when her father came south, he worked as a French polisher. 'He worked with very grand people who had good furniture. He worked for years for the O'Connor Dunnes in Castlerea, they were the last of the Connaught kings. They wouldn't let anyone in to touch the furniture, only Dad.' But his furniture skills didn't extend to his own house. 'As Mum would say, the chair could fall from under you and he wouldn't fix it. That was the funny part of it.'

Pauline has vivid memories of going to school. 'There was one nun, and you would shake going in in the morning if you had her. She was a terror. The contrariest woman. The majority of the nuns were quite nice, but they always took the wealthier students up to the top of the class, we poor ones were put at the back, and the poorer you were, you were nearly out the back door. There was awful favouritism. My two eldest sisters, Patricia and Loreto, they hated school. They always came home and complained, but they were divils, they wouldn't do the homework. But myself, Éamonn and Philomena, the three youngest, we would do our homework and we couldn't understand why the other two girls weren't getting on with the nuns.'

The majority of the nuns were
quite nice, but they always took the
wealthier students up to the top of
the class, we poor ones were put at
the back, and the poorer you were,
you were nearly out the back door.

Pauline left the convent school at fourteen and went to the vocational school for two years. 'I was sent in to study for office work, and I thought to myself, *No, I won't be sitting behind a desk all day, I wouldn't like it.* So I went in for domestic science. I learned quite a bit and saw a few things that poor Mother didn't have in the kitchen.'

Falling in Love and Marrying Young

After she left the vocational school, Pauline stayed at home to help out. Then she met her husband, Hugh. 'I used to have to pass his house when I was going to school. And he said he clapped his eye on me when I was passing, and sure I hadn't a clue who he was.'

This was during the war years, and Hugh was

Pauline's daughters, Dympna, Olivia and Pauline.

the Post Office Linesman. 'That was his title. The war affected it anyway and he was let go. There was no work in Castlerea, it was never a great place for work. He signed up with some crowd that was taking names of Irish lads to send them to work in England. This was in the 1940s. He was picked, and, of course, we were in love by this time. We thought about what would happen if he was killed in England. There were so many of our neighbours getting wounded, so and so was killed in the raid, all that. So he says, "We'll get married." So we did get married and I wasn't fully eighteen. We got married in April, and I wasn't eighteen until June.'

Pauline says her parents took it well. 'They

were disappointed, but they never kicked up a row about it or ran us down but we stuck together and we were together over sixty-three years before he died.'

It's fifteen years now and it's amazing, there are nights when I'll wake up, and, just for a split second, I'll imagine his head is on the pillow beside me. I do talk to him, I give out to him, so I do. I still feel very close to him, especially since I lost my daughter.

Hugh died in 2004. 'It's fifteen years now and it's amazing, there are nights when I'll wake up, and, just for a split second, I'll imagine his head is on the pillow beside me. I do talk to him, I give out to him, so I do. I still feel very close to him, especially since I lost my daughter. I had three daughters in my marriage, Dympna, Olivia and Pauline, and he always thought that the next one was going to be a boy. We never got the boy. After Pauline was born,

Pauline and Hughie
Hilliard and daughters.
Dympna's Communion
1954.

he said, "Well, that's it, I'm hanging up my boots." I said, "It makes no difference wearing the boots or anything else, you still got your daughters."

What's in a Name?

'Wait till I tell you about Pauline. In those days, the mum never got out of bed for nine days after the birth, with the result that I was never at any of my children's christenings. So Hughie and the godmother and godfather went off to get Pauline christened. "Now, Hughie," I said, "remember, its Grace Maria I want her christened." "I won't forget," says he.

'So they got to the church all right, but the mistake I made was I hadn't told the godparents or written it down. So when it came to christening the child, Hughie forgot Grace Maria, and the priest suggested to call her after her mother. And that is why Pauline is Pauline! We laughed over it. It's funny, every time we meet a person that is Grace, I say to Pauline, "That should be your name."'

Emigration – and a Stroke of Luck

After the children were born, work was still scarce, so Pauline and Hugh headed to England, leaving the three girls in the care of Pauline's mother. 'We did very well in England. We were nine years there. I worked too, and was very pleased with myself. Office work first, in a banking office of a big clothing firm. I always dealt with money. I have handled millions, and not a penny of it my own. And then I got into the post office, not on the counters but in the office with the money.'

Hughie worked for the Central Electricity Board, which provided them with a house. Then he was asked to leave London. 'I said no. I was used to London at that stage and the girls were used to it.' Their three daughters had joined their parents when they had got settled in England.

Then they had a wonderful stroke of luck. 'Hughie always did the pools, and he was very lucky one weekend, he got four or five thousand pounds. That was a lot of money in those days.' So on the strength of that they were able to return to Ireland and buy a house. They bought a house in Navan, where the family has lived for fifty-two years.

Hughie always did the pools, and he was very lucky one weekend, he got four or five thousand pounds.

'I was used to my wages in England, and we came home and there was no work. Then the Greyhound Board, Bord na gCon, was setting up. Now I didn't know the first thing about a greyhound from beginning to end, his head could be where his tail should be, but they were giving great money and it was only a part-time job, a few hours an evening twice or three times a week. It was the best-paid part-time job in the country.'

Death of a Daughter

Pauline's second girl, Olivia, died from breast cancer. 'That was in 2008, she was just coming on to sixty. She had two boys. It nearly killed me.

Olivia died on the first of August and, in January 2009, I was complaining of shooting pains in my body. I was sent to Blanchardstown Hospital for tests and I was diagnosed with cancer of the bowel.

'I had three operations within three weeks, with the result that I was out of this world for two months. I didn't know what was going on, and, along with that, I was completely crippled. I died three times, so I did. I can still remember those times when I would be asleep or dreaming or whatever, and there was this big white tunnel. Oh, it was snow white. And every time I would come near it I would say, "No, no, no." And they were wondering what all my "No, no, nos" were, because they didn't realise, they couldn't see what I was seeing. Three times, it happened. They thought I was dead. The last time it happened ... I have a little altar at home where I lived before I came in here [Woodlands Nursing Home in Navan], and at the end of this white tunnel was my little altar. But it still didn't bring me into it. I survived. I was six months altogether in the hospital. It took two months of exercise and all that to get me moving again.'

'I'm Going To Be Buried Beside My Husband'

Pauline is not happy with the state of her country today. 'It frightens me. It just frightens me, and I feel so upset, worried for my grandchildren, my great-grandchildren. It is a different world. It is not Ireland any longer and I won't be sorry to say goodbye to it.'

> It just frightens me, and I feel so
> upset, worried for my grandchildren,
> my great-grandchildren. It is a
> different world. It is not Ireland any
> longer and I won't be sorry to
> say goodbye to it.

And what advice would this mother, grandmother and great-grandmother offer to young people today? 'My advice to them – and I don't know if it is the right advice or not – is try and always be human. No matter who you meet, they are a human being. And never do anything to anyone or anything that you wouldn't do to yourself.'

She retains her faith, despite some misgivings about the Church. 'The religious have no one to blame only themselves because they let the clergy get away with so much damage. The nuns and the priests. The abuse. The child abuse. They knew they would get away with it. I haven't that much respect for the Catholic Church, but my faith is stronger than ever. It is between me and the man above now.'

She considers herself to be a religious person and believes in an afterlife. 'Oh definitely. If you didn't have that bit of a belief, what's the point? I have planned my own funeral, I have instructions left for them. I have a grandson who looks after me here, and his wife. She is only a granddaughter-in-law to me but they are marvellous. They know my plans but if there is anything there that doesn't suit them, I'll be gone, so I won't worry. I'm going to be buried beside my husband.'

And what does she think about death? 'My life here – I have no control over anything. I can't make plans to do anything. I would go in the morning if He called me. I have had a queer life. My mother was such a great woman, she had a leg amputated when she was eighty-six. She lived until she was ninety-four. Dad was never a hefty man, he died at sixty-seven. I keep saying to myself, *I'll get to ninety-four*. I wouldn't ask to live to be a hundred.

Spreading the Turf

James Mullin
Born 13 September 1927

Australia, Canada, America, New Zealand, England – James Mullin reels off the places he has worked around the world. But he was born in the tiny village of Slieve, outside Dunmore in County Galway, one of thirteen children of Luke and Margaret Mullin. 'There were twelve boys and one girl and I was the fourth in the family. My father was a farmer. He used to sow bits of things. We all helped on the farm, and we used to go to the bog spreading turf. Dad used to cut it with a *sleán*. There was no machinery on the bog then. We would have a barrow with maybe six or nine sods in the barrow and we would tip it and make rows. And then we would collect it. It was a very simple life.'

James at Central Park Nursing Home near Ballinasloe, where he now lives, 2019.

Most of the food for the family was produced on their own farm and the favourite meal was bacon and cabbage with their own home-reared pig.

Antipodes Bound

Eventually, the large brood began to drift away from home. James left school at fourteen and went to work on the farm alongside his father. Then he got itchy feet too, and, at seventeen, took the boat to England where he took up a labouring job on the building sites. While he was there, he saw an advertisement for work in Australia and applied for that.

He got the job and remembers that his ticket cost him ten pounds. 'And it took me five weeks and three days to get there by boat. We went ashore at every station for an hour or two so we saw a bit of the world as well.'

For work in Australia, James drove a bulldozer. 'Then I joined the railways in Sydney, and they asked if I would like to become a train examiner. I said yes and so they trained us in and brought us around the train, and then brought us into a room to do a test. I passed the test. "It's all for safety," they told us. "You have to make sure the brakes are all okay and the pistons are working. When you test a train out, if you make a mistake and someone gets killed, you can serve ten years in jail." So I was *very* careful.'

> It took me five weeks and three days
> to get there by boat. We went ashore
> at every station for an hour or two so
> we saw a bit of the world as well.

Later James moved to New Zealand and, while living in Auckland, he got to know a man, Frederick Foster, who was later convicted for the murder of a young woman. Foster was executed on 7 June 1955. Only four more men would be executed in New Zealand before the death penalty was abolished.

And having worked in so many places, he says he is glad he came home. 'It was important to me. I met some fellas, especially one young lad, and I said, "Will you come back?" And he said, "No, I'm staying here." And I said, "Well, I'm coming back." And I left him there.'

And his advice to young people today? 'Travel a bit, have a look around the world. See a bit of the world.'

1928: Major Events

World

- First appearance of Walt Disney's Mickey Mouse

- Alexander Fleming discovers penicillin

- D.H. Lawrence's *Lady Chatterley's Lover* is banned in the UK and the USA

- First home pregnancy kit is introduced in France

- Che Guevara, Ariel Sharon and Shirley Temple are born

Ireland

- The first East–West transatlantic flight leaves Baldonnel aerodrome in Dublin; Commandant James Fitzmaurice is on board the *Bremen*

- The foundation stone of the new Northern Ireland parliament building is laid at Stormont

- It is suggested that the old Irish flag – that of a gold harp with a blue background – should be carried at the Olympic Games in Amsterdam; however, the Irish Tricolour has already been registered as the national flag

- The Tricolour is raised for the first time at the Games when Dr Pat O'Callaghan wins a gold medal for hammer-throwing

- The first Irish coinage is circulated in the state

- Irish becomes a compulsory subject for the Intermediate Certificate

- Albanian missionary sister Agnes Gonxha Bojaxhiu, later known as Mother Teresa, joins the Sisters of Loreto at Loreto Abbey, Rathfarnham, to learn English in order to teach schoolchildren in India

- The Gate Theatre in Dublin is founded by English actors Micheál Mac Liammóir and Hilton Edwards

- The tenor John McCormack is appointed a papal count for his services to music

- All-Ireland champions: Cork (hurling) and Kildare (football)

Memories of Eviction
Michael O'Connell
Born 12 April 1928

'My parents were John and Ellen O'Connell (née Molan); Molan was probably a common name around Mitchelstown, that was the area she came from. My grandmother was evicted in the late 1800s from the farm they had there. She came to live in Cork with her mother, in a house on the South Douglas Road and that's the house I was born in.'

Today, Michael lives in an apartment with the Little Sisters of the Poor in Roebuck, Dublin, and, coincidently, one of his friends there is Denis O'Callaghan, who appears elsewhere in this book. He was also born in Cork, went to the same schools and also joined the civil service. 'Actually the very first day that I came in here, Denis came in and I recognised him straight away and I made myself known,' says Michael. 'It's nice to have someone to talk to, we look after ourselves, it's independent living.'

A Rambling Boy

'My father was a draper's assistant in Grants in Cork but they were actually farming people, there were five or six siblings. The earliest memory I have is from when I was three or four years old. On this particular day, I rambled out of our house and up the road for whatever particular reason, I was mooching. I rambled to a house less than half a mile away up the back Douglas road, that was in the morning. I remember I had a very happy time there, I don't know what I was doing there, but I was comfortable and happy. But it came time to come home … I don't remember coming home, but I know it was about four o'clock, and when I got home my mother was distraught. "Where had I been all the day, like?"

'It is a recollection that comes into my head frequently because it recalls Jesus in the temple in Jerusalem, and the distraught Mary looking for him.'

Michael had two brothers. The eldest Sean died

eight years ago and his younger brother Noel died in 1991. 'He was an engineer, he went to college in UCC.'

Michael's long memory encompasses his early schooldays. 'The first school I went to was the South Presentation Convent on Evergreen Street in Cork, a little school. I don't remember the boys who were in the class with me, but I remember Miss Tarrant, one of the teachers. And there was a nun there. And I made my First Communion there. Then, at the age of seven, there was the end of that and we had to go down to the Christian Brothers in Sullivan's Quay. It would have been about a mile away from my home so we walked there.'

Michael says that when he left school he wanted to get a job. 'That would have been mainly what people wanted at that time. It was 1945. Jobs were so scarce. I had done the Leaving Cert. You could go as far as Inter Cert with the Christian Brothers then you had to go on to North Monastery if you wanted to do the Leaving Cert. It was just beyond the North Cathedral, a bit of a foreign part for people from our side of town.'

Around the Country with the Civil Service

Michael decided to take the civil service clerical officer exam, having been foiled in his ambition to go to UCC. 'You couldn't go to college at that time unless you had money, and my father was just an ordinary draper's assistant – and I had a young brother coming up behind me. So I did the exam and got fourteenth place.'

At that time, you got to nominate which department you wanted to work in. 'Because there was a tax office in Cork, I thought that I would like to be a member of the Revenue Commissioners. As a tax officer, there was a slightly better pay scale than a general civil servant. So then next thing, I was appointed to Castlebar. And for a Cork City young fella, being appointed to Castlebar in 1945, it was like being sent to America. And the trains were only run on wet turf at the time, it would take you two days to get to Castlebar. So I said, "Oh Jesus, I can't." So I made representations to the civil service commissioner myself, as a seventeen-year-old, and I was told that they had made this appointment and it couldn't be changed. And I said, "Well, I can't go to Castlebar." Eventually, they relented and appointed me to the Land Commission and I became a clerical officer in Merrion Square in Dublin.'

And for a Cork City young fella, being appointed to Castlebar in 1945, it was like being sent to America.

Michael heard later that the Inspector of Taxes in Castlebar, Tom Tuohy, was at the station in the town waiting for this young fella to arrive but he never did. After six years in Dublin, Michael was appointed to Cork, where he remained for ten years, then back to Dublin, then Waterford for seventeen years, where he was in charge of the tax office. Then he got a further promotion and went back to Dublin where he became Principal Inspector of Taxes. 'It was tough making all those moves, sometimes it involved selling a house and getting a new house. And you got ten days' notice. It was a monastic kind of set-up.'

Michael and Thérese.

An Office Romance

Michael met Thérèse Halliden, his wife-to-be, in the tax office in Cork where they worked together. I remark that I didn't think office romances would have been encouraged back then. 'There was no question of encouragement, really. They weren't aware of it first and then they didn't give a damn. It was a fraught romance in many ways because she had been connected with another guy in the office.'

'So she was two-timing you?'

'She wasn't two-timing me, she was two timing *the other guy*! I wasn't in any position to tell her to make up her mind, she was holding all the cards. So a very good friend of mine, Edward Murray, he was concerned about the situation and filled me in.

But it made no difference, I proceeded anyway and that was it.'

The couple tied the knot in 1955. 'We got married in Kanturk, which is where she was living at the time. In the beginning of 1954, she was struck by a car when she was crossing the road and she was out of action for six or seven months. She was living at home with her parents. Her father was a TD, P.J. Halliden, a member of the Farmers' Party.'

The late Patrick Joseph Halliden was a Clann na Talmhan deputy. A farmer and teacher by profession, he was first elected to Dáil Éireann for the Cork North constituency at the 1943 general election and was re-elected in 1944 and 1948, after which, he retired from politics.

The wedding took place in the Hibernian Hotel in Mallow. 'We had about forty people there. The honeymoon was in a little town called Esbly, about thirty kilometres east of Paris. We flew, the first time I ever flew, from Dublin to London and stayed in London a few days, and then we got the boat over to France. What happened was Thérèse's brother, he was a Columban priest, and he was a professor in Dalgan Park, with the result that he had this lovely three months in the middle of summer, like all teachers, and what he used to do was do locum for the parish priest in Esbly.'

Michael and Thérèse stayed in a house belonging to her brother's friends. 'We were royally entertained. They insisted on us coming down for the evening meal every day. It was very plentiful but the thing about it was that Thérèse wasn't a big eater at the time as she was recovering from the accident, and I felt it incumbent upon myself to eat everything that was put in front of me in case there was any offence taken. After three days, I was bloated, and I said, "I can't stick this. Tell them I have a *mal de ventre*, a tummy ache."'

Memories of Thérèse

Eventually the couple settled in Blackrock. 'We had no children; nieces and nephews, yes.'

Thérèse died in 1999. 'She was young enough. I stayed on living in the house we bought in Blackrock, until I decided a couple of years ago that I wasn't looking forward to another winter by myself, I was beginning to lose a bit of energy, and I was okay to make meals. She was a very good cook and I learned a lot from her, I could cook for myself quite competently, but that involves going and buying the bloody stuff and then you have to cook the stuff and then you have to eat the stuff and then you have to wash up the stuff and then you have to think about what you're going to have tomorrow. Then I had a little knock or two and I said, "I better do something, change my lifestyle", and I came in here.'

> I could cook for myself quite
> competently, but that involves going
> and buying the bloody stuff and then
> you have to cook the stuff and then
> you have to eat the stuff and then
> you have to wash up the stuff and
> then you have to think about what
> you're going to have tomorrow.

Michael misses his wife very much. 'She was very talented in many ways. She was very talented at embroidery, she was good at the piano. A perfectionist in one way; if she hit a wrong note she would stop and I would say, "Keep going."

Thérèse was also an artist. 'In my room up there, I have a load of her pictures and I look at them every day and say, "Cripes, they're good." There's one picture, it wouldn't be her best, it is a picture of the River Suir and trees, and actually it is four miles from where we lived in Waterford. There was a pub there, a great music place. And we were passing down near there once and Thérèse said, "That is where I would like to be buried, with the lovely view."' It wasn't to be her final resting place but the picture holds great memories for Michael.

Michael is also an author, having penned two books in recent years. The first was a history of the Church of Saint John the Baptist in Blackrock in County Dublin, which was blessed and dedicated in September 1945. In his introduction, Michael writes:

> *What seemed in the beginning a humdrum task of research into the history of our church turned into a treasure hunt in the social and general history of the mid 19th and 20th centuries, and the emergence of many outstanding personages, largely unknown now, but important in their time. Their names and stories covered by the sands of time, uncovered now, to the delight of lovers of Blackrock.*

Michael has also written *The Martins of Lisieux*,

which tells the story of St Thérèse of Lisieux as well as that of her extended family. In his account of the canonisation of St Thérèse's parents, Louis and Zélie, on 18 October 2015, Michael quotes the words of Pope Francis, who said: 'Remember this: Blessed Louis Martin and Blessed Zélie Guérin were not canonised because of their daughter Saint Thérèse – she was canonised because of them.'

Quo Vadis?

So what does Michael think of Ireland today? 'I think it is bloody awful. It's not the Ireland that I grew up in. The values that we had, that we learned, of chivalry, honesty, pride in our history and our country, that's not there anymore. It is not the Ireland that I loved as a young person. I'm not a member of a political party but I will vote. I'm horrified at the way the "group think" has taken over in the media.'

I think it is bloody awful. It's not the Ireland that I grew up in. The values that we had, that we learned, of chivalry, honesty, pride in our history and our country, that's not there anymore.

Michael is a religious person. 'I don't get annoyed, but ... people say, "Oh I'm not religious, but I am spiritual." What the hell do they mean? Why are we ashamed of saying we are religious in this country? It is nothing to be ashamed of.' He hopes that the faith won't be lost in the years ahead. 'People will begin to wake up sometime.'

And what of an afterlife? Will we meet up with our loved ones again? 'I think that part of it is actually oversold, because that is not what we are going up there for. I'm not going up to meet Thérèse only, and all the pals I had, I am going up there to meet the Lord, which is very difficult to explain or sell to anyone.'

And is he afraid of death? 'I wouldn't be looking forward to a painful death but the actual process, no. I have had a lot of pals that have gone through it. At least they've done it, so I can do it too.'

1929: Major Events

World

- The Wall Street Crash in the USA leads to the Great Depression

- Seven members and associates of Chicago's North Side Gang are murdered in what would become known as the St Valentine's Day Massacre; the incident is related to rivalry between Al Capone and Bugs Moran

- The Vatican City State gains independence from Italy

- The first Academy Awards (Oscars), held at the Hollywood Roosevelt Hotel, are hosted by Douglas Fairbanks Snr

- Grace Kelly, Anne Frank, Jacqueline Kennedy Onassis and Audrey Hepburn are born

Ireland

- All cats from abroad, except Great Britain, are to be kept in quarantine for a period of six months to prevent rabies

- A Belfast court sentences Fianna Fáil leader Éamon de Valera to one month in jail for illegally entering County Armagh

- Major-General Seán Mac Eoin, the 'Blacksmith of Ballinalee', is appointed Chief of Staff of the army

- Maud Gonne MacBride is arrested and charged with seditious libel against the state

- Some 300,000 people attend the pontifical high mass at the Phoenix Park to mark the end of the Catholic Emancipation centenary celebrations

- The restored General Post Office in Dublin is officially opened by President W.T. Cosgrave

- The Shannon hydro-electric scheme at Ardnacrusha, County Clare, is completed following seven years' construction

- Elizabeth Bowen publishes her novel *The Last September*, set during the Irish War of Independence

- All-Ireland champions: Cork (hurling) and Kerry (football)

A Border Crossing

Austin Dawe
Born 10 January 1929

When your father was Felix Dawe, the Vice-Commander of a battalion of the Irish Republican Army, that gives you a little spot in the history of your town. Austin Dawe was born in the border town of Dundalk, County Louth, to Felix and Mary (neé McEwen). 'I grew up in the steam age,' he says, 'and when we were children, it was great to get up in the morning and look out the window and see the ships in the bay, you could see them, all the smoke coming up. You could see the smoke before you saw the boat. Dundalk was a busy port then, there would be three or four boats with every tide, lots of them bringing in coal.'

Dundalk was a busy port then, there
would be three or four boats with
every tide, lots of them
bringing in coal.

Felix Dawe and the IRA

When Austin was born, his father Felix was
involved in what his son describes as 'illegal
activity', although he never spoke about it to
his family. Nevertheless, Austin always knew his
father was in the IRA and Vice-Commander of
the Fourth Northern Division under Frank Aiken,
who later served as a government minister and as
Tánaiste from 1965 to 1969.

He had been involved in an incident at the RIC
barracks in Greenore in 1921. He was recognised
by someone who said, 'Oh, you're young Dawes
from across the wall. Mum's the word. We'll be all
right and you'll be all right but any guns you have,
we want them.' So that was that.'

Felix was eventually captured and held in the
jail in Dundalk. On 27 July 1922, there was a
breakout by anti-Treaty forces; a device exploded
against the jail wall, leaving a gap through which

Take-over of GREENORE R.I.C. BARRACKS. March 1922.

HUGHIE	BARNEY	JIMMY	FELIX DAWE	JIMMY	– BOYLE	JACK
TRAYNOR	CARROLL	MORAN	Cooley	MEEGAN	Greenore	FLOOD
Dundalk	Dundalk	Dundalk		Inniskeen		Dundalk

Photo donated 1973 by:
Miss Rory Hall, Dundalk via her nephew Sean Hall

Felix Dawe, Austin's father, (centre) at the takeover of
Greenore RIC Barracks, March 1922.

the prisoners could make a run for it. One hundred
and six prisoners escaped; many were re-captured,
but Felix remained free.

'The escape was premeditated and planned,'
says Austin. 'At the time, there was a priest who
loaned my father a suit and a car to escape out of
the town. And I think the priest was shifted after it
was discovered he was helping the prisoners, doing
the right thing at the wrong time. He was shifted
away to Australia.'

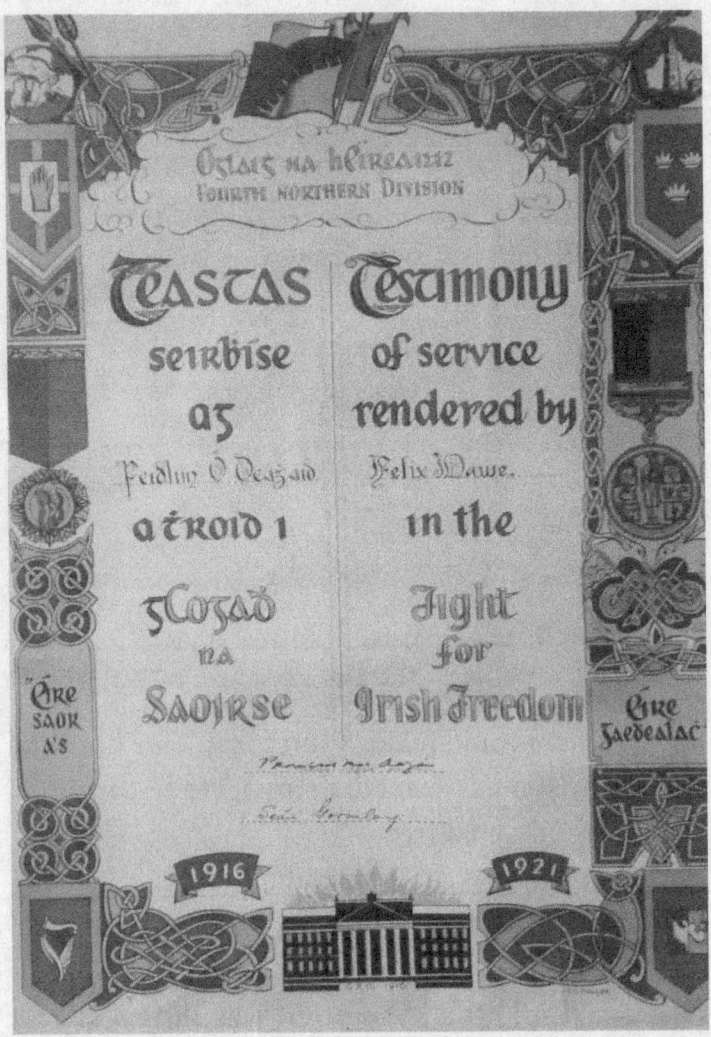

Certificate awarded to Felix Dawe for his services with the Fourth Northern Division of the Old IRA, signed by Frank Aiken.

Today, Felix is commemorated in the list of escapees on the wall of the jail.

> At the time, there was a priest who
> loaned my father a suit and a car
> to escape out of the town. And I
> think the priest was shifted after it
> was discovered he was helping the
> prisoners, doing the right thing at the
> wrong time. He was shifted away
> to Australia.

Austin also remembers when the military service pensions were being allotted and 'there were a lot of different people coming and saying they did this and that'. But Austin was never political. 'I never got involved in anything like that. I lived a quiet, peaceful life within my means.'

Farming the Land in Bellurgan

The Dawes grew up on a farm in Bellurgan, about five or six miles from the border with Northern Ireland. Austin's father came from a farming family and his mother Mary was a tailoress. Her father was a tailor too, and Austin remembers that he wore a bowler hat and had a rocking chair.

Austin was one of eight children, he himself was born a twin but his sister Dolores died some years ago. In Bellurgan, farming was carried out in a community spirit. 'We had a farm but no machines or anything, the neighbours used to come in and break up the land and sow the crops to keep us going over the winter.' And then he was working in the alcohol factory. 'I remember the black scab coming in the area, on the potatoes.'

During the war years, the family cut turf for fuel. 'We used to go up with the donkey and cart, over as far as the mountain and walk up. Sure the whole country was cutting turf. Whole families went. You'd get a bit of land, the width of this room, and cut it up and spread it out and it would lay out for a week or so and you'd have to stack it up. We enjoyed it anyway, anything was better than going to school. We would have supplies and a picnic on the mountainside.'

Crossing the Border

Austin was about fourteen before he crossed the border into the North. He was in an athletic club in Bellurgan, and went to the All-Ireland Cross-Country Championship. 'It would have been held in Belfast and you needed visas to go there. Vincent Mulligan was over the club at the time and he asked me to collect the visas.

'So I got a lend of a bicycle and went over the border on it. Down at the bottom of Newry Hill, there were four RUC men walking along; I was on this side of the road and they were on the other. There were very bad brakes on the bike and Newry Hill is about three miles long. So I got off the bike and walked across and excused myself and said, "Could you tell me where the RUC station is?" And your man was in a giddy mood and he says, "Why, do you want to give yourself up?" He was a nice man. I said I had been sent on a mission to get these visas for the All-Ireland in Belfast, so he directed me to the station and I went down, and they were very nice; I had nothing to hide and they had nothing to hide. Incidentally, we went down to Belfast that day, and my eyes were opened with the amount of military equipment that was about. It was serious, guns and armoured cars everywhere. I always remember that J.J. Barry from Tipperary won the All-Ireland Athletics.'

Austin and
Charlotte's wedding,
1950.

The Perfect Fit

Austin went to work in Clarks shoe factory on Quay Street in Dundalk. But the arrival of seven new workers one morning was to change his life. 'I was infatuated by a woman called Charlotte. Seven or eight of them started that morning, punched in and somehow or other, she stood out.' Charlotte McGrath was one of fourteen children and the daughter of a carriage painter on the GNR Railway in Dundalk.

However, things were complicated. 'She was going out with a boy at that time,' says Austin.

A couple of years later, however, Charlotte asked her friend to tell Austin that she would be very interested in a friendship with him, and so Austin and Charlotte made an 'appointment' for the following Saturday night to go to the

Redemptorist Novena in St Patrick's. 'It was the thing to do at the time. We were more religious and innocent, you know.' The couple went out for about four years before they married in 1950. Austin remembers proposing to Charlotte when he was twenty-two. 'I said you don't have to answer me yet, tell me whenever. And I was delighted when she said yes.

'We had no money and we decided, for our marrying year, we wouldn't go to the pictures, plays or dances, and we put our spending money aside for the rainy day. We walked every highway and byway and cycled every road and had a lovely time. People used to say, "Why didn't you go here or there?" but we were just doing our own thing.'

The following year, during their two weeks' holidays, they decided to go to Lough Derg. 'That was when the train was going from Dundalk to Bundoran. They were telling us before we went how hard it was going to be, so we were waiting the whole time for the hard part; it was lovely weather while we were there. And the next thing it was all over. We arrived home and people were saying, "You didn't go to Lough Derg at all, you went to Bundoran for the weekend!" They had their own thoughts.'

They went back to Lough Derg the next year but it proved to be a very different and difficult experience. 'See, you went round in your bare feet, and the stones were very sharp. For a bit of comfort, there was a sandy patch and you could dabble your feet in the water, but then, when you went up and walked around the basilica, you were leaving sand and it was sore when you would kneel down on the kneeling board with sand all over it. We got black tea and you had a certain number of stations you had to do, you didn't get any sleep at all the first night. In the morning, after being awake all night with different prayers and sermons, it was very hard. The whole thing was to keep yourself awake and not let yourself drift away. The second day you didn't have to do as much, it was just a matter of staying. If the weather was nice, you could get into a nice warm spot and enjoy the sun but if it was cold and wet, it was miserable.'

> In the morning, after being awake
> all night with different prayers and
> sermons, it was very hard. The whole
> thing was to keep yourself awake and
> not let yourself drift away.

Finding a Home and Starting a Musical Family

Austin says it was just as hard for a young couple to get a house then as it is now.

Their first attempt at renting fell flat when the owners of the house decided they wanted to sell it instead. The family, from Liverpool, had tried living there but they only lasted a few weeks. 'It was out in the country and they were used to having a shop next door to them, but they were two miles away from the shop, and they would sit down for their tea, and discover they had no milk, and they'd have to get the bike and go to the shop, and then they would discover they had no sugar or something.'

Austin and Charlotte were about to rent the house for ten shillings a week when the rug was pulled from under them and the house went on the market for five hundred pounds. Austin's wages at the time were two pounds ten shillings a week. 'The rent was within our means. I could visualise myself working in the garden and I thought I would be able to keep chickens.'

So instead, the couple got a small plot of land and made a makeshift place for a time. 'We built it ourselves. Then a house became available in Dundalk and we decided we would move to town. At that point, we'd had the first baby, Diana, and we decided if we were living in town, it would be handy for school and the chapel and all, so we moved.' Austin describes how they went on to have seven children, one for each day of the week, three boys and four girls: Diana, Gerarde, Itamonica (RIP), Austin, Sinead, Dermot and Muriel. Charlotte died in 1995.

This is a musical family. Gerarde, Austin Junior and Dermot all played traditional music and all four girls were classical piano players and played trad as well. Austin Junior was a renowned fiddle player with Comhaltas Ceoltóirí Éireann and the Fiddlers of Oriel. But, in 2009, he had a bad fall while putting up the Christmas lights in his home and sustained seventy-four fractures and had to spend three weeks in a coma, and one hundred days in hospital in total. He damaged his hand, which means he is now unable to play his beloved fiddle.

Austin Senior is a lifelong pioneer. He has never tasted alcohol, and never smoked, he is still driving and is an active member of Inniskeen Pitch and Putt Club. He never misses nine o'clock mass in St Nicholas Church where he is still an active collector and parish worker.

When Clarks shoe factory closed in 1985, he retrained as a bus driver and worked with Anchor Tours, Bellurgan. He then went on to deliver home heating oil before retiring in his seventies.

The Ireland of Today and the World Beyond

Austin has strong views on the state of Ireland ninety years after his birth. 'Ireland is a lovely place, we made a name for ourselves everywhere we went, we captured the American hearts. The Irish have always been very good. The only thing that annoys me from time to time, especially now, is our friends in the North. They have England in an awful state and England can't see what's happening. They would build a ship, for example, make an estimate, halfway through they run out of money and the English would bail them out. They eventually closed down the shipyard.

The only thing that annoys me
from time to time, especially now,
is our friends in the North. They
have England in an awful state and
England can't see what's happening.

'I thought that [Theresa] May was a good politician and doing her best, but you see them over there in England, fighting like cats and dogs, and they don't know what they're fighting about. People down here in the south are laughing at them, because they only want one thing – the Good Friday Agreement done away with.'

During the Troubles, he says, you knew different people that were doing different things but you would pass no remarks, that was their business. 'There was no trouble where I lived. You had to go out of your way to make trouble.'

Over the past fifteen years, Austin has become an intrepid traveller. His first holiday was to South Africa where Diana, his eldest daughter, is married to a vet. But persuading Austin and Charlotte to undertake the trip wasn't that easy. It was done through a family friend, Fr McGrew, who met Diana in South Africa and relayed the invitation to her parents. 'Go down to the Fairgreen,' she told the priest, 'and invite Daddy and Mammy to come to South Africa, and don't leave until you get a definite answer.'

'So we went and we had a great holiday beyond with Diana and David in Johannesburg. I think we were there for seven weeks.' And their travels continued, with further holidays in France, South America, the USA, Canada and Australia.

'I Go to Confession, I Keep the Slate Clean'

Austin believes in God, in education and in music. 'Music is an international language and you are welcome anywhere if you can play a tune or sing a song.'

And although he is happy with Ireland generally, he is very disappointed with the number of people who are not practising their religion. 'There were a lot of unfortunate incidents where the priests and bishops were abusing their positions and that had its effect on a lot of people. But if you take a barrel of apples and there's one bad one, you would throw it away. You wouldn't throw away all the good ones as well.'

Austin goes to mass each morning and he believes there is an afterlife. 'It's going to be nice. It's very simple, you have to believe in something. Just look out the window there and sure who is looking after the grass, the birds? Somebody is.' He is very accepting of death. 'When you get to ninety, you have seen a lot of people die, you've lost a lot of your family. We're getting into troubled waters now! Death is something that comes. A lot of people die young but a lot of older people like myself, God wants us here.'

And Austin makes his own preparations. 'I go to confession, I keep the slate clean.'

Acknowledgements

At the heart of this book are twenty-six nonagenarians who shared their memories with me. Meeting them and spending time with them has left me happy, humbled and in awe of their spirit and their experience. What their eyes have seen and their ears have heard is precious and I have been fortunate to listen to their joys and tragedies, the stories of their families and their first-hand accounts of history before it became history. There were lovely moments when they shared old letters and photo albums and remembered family long gone and schooldays long spent.

I enjoyed great hospitality on my travels, warm fires, homemade scones, friendship. It was a fascinating time, travelling around meeting people, drinking tea and having the chats! I want to thank all of the participants and the friends and family who volunteered them to take part. These include Sandra Crosby of St Francis Nursing Home, Mount Oliver, Dundalk; Diane Jones of Woodlands House Nursing Home in Navan; Rois McDonagh of Central Park Nursing Home in Clonberne, Ballinasloe; Jackie Haskins of Retreat Nursing Home in Athlone, and Deirdre Moore of Padre Pio Nursing Home in Holycross. Also, Michael McGlynn of Nursing Homes Ireland whose organisation compiled *A Story I have lived so long to make*, a series of inspirational writings from nursing-home residents.

Thank you to those who sourced old photographs, who scoured attics and shoeboxes and old handbags, and to Ruth McCormack for her help in getting the text ready for the publisher. And for the science bit – the number crunching – thank you to Marie Crowley of the Vital Statistics Archive in the Central Statistics Office.

The idea for the book came from my editor at Hachette Ireland, Ciara Considine, who was a constant inspiration and support – thank you, Ciara. Thank you also to Joanna Smyth and the team at Hachette Ireland, copy-editor Aonghus Meaney and proofreader Claire Rourke.

I also had great support from my family and especially my husband, Brian, my constant companion on my travels. Thank you all.

The publisher would like to thank Nick Bradshaw for permission to reproduce the image of Cyril Galbraith on page 179, and all of the interviewees and their families for permission to reproduce the featured images.